The New York Times

IN THE KITCHEN CROSSWORDS
75 Easy-to-Challenging Puzzles

Edited by Will Shortz

ST. MARTIN'S GRIFFIN ☙ NEW YORK

THE NEW YORK TIMES IN THE KITCHEN CROSSWORDS.
Copyright © 2008 by The New York Times Company. All rights reserved.
Printed in the United States of America. For information, address
St. Martin's Press, 175 Fifth Avenue, New York, N.Y. 10010.

www.stmartins.com

All of the puzzles that appear in this work were originally published
in the *New York Times* from August 13, 2007, to November 16, 2007.
Copyright © 2007 by The New York Times Company.
All rights reserved. Reprinted by permission.

ISBN-13: 978-0-312-38259-9
ISBN-10: 0-312-38259-6

First Edition: July 2008

10 9 8 7 6 5 4 3 2 1

The New York Times

IN THE KITCHEN CROSSWORDS

ACROSS

1 Town known for witch trials
6 ___-friendly
10 Jane Austen heroine
14 Politician who wrote "The Audacity of Hope"
15 Senate errand runner
16 Authentic
17 Fortune-seeking trio
19 Formerly
20 Hrs. in a Yankee schedule
21 Mimicked
22 Feels sorry for
24 Hits the roof
26 Brought to ruin
27 Barely make, with "out"
28 Peru-Bolivia border lake
31 Mosey along
34 Walnut or willow
35 Oozy roofing material
36 Grass-eating trio
40 One of the Manning quarterbacks
41 Giant birds of lore
42 Brain sections
43 Pedestrian's intersection warning
46 Soccer Hall of Famer Hamm
47 Exclamations of annoyance
48 Took a load off one's feet
52 Respectful tribute
54 War on drugs fighter
55 China's Chairman ___

56 Enthusiastic
57 Gift-giver's trio
60 Frilly material
61 Pint, inch or second
62 Bird on the Great Seal of the United States
63 Ran away from
64 Turner of "Peyton Place," 1957
65 Sticks around

DOWN

1 They're always underfoot
2 Put up with
3 Coffee concoction
4 Aid provider to the critically injured, briefly
5 "Nonsense!"
6 Increased
7 Uttered
8 Omelet ingredient
9 Peaceful interludes
10 Titillating
11 Trio at sea
12 Riot-control spray
13 Draft picks in pubs
18 Fencing sword
23 Amin of Africa
25 Peddle
26 Food regimens
28 Racecourse
29 Casual eatery
30 Obedience school sounds
31 In the sack
32 Venus de ___
33 Trio on the run
34 Hammers and hoes
37 Appreciative
38 Minor hang-ups
39 Highway or byway
44 Sent to another team
45 Jokester
46 Painter Chagall
48 December list keeper
49 Alpha's opposite
50 In a weak manner
51 Sniffers
52 50%
53 Football-shaped
54 Dresden denial
58 Cell's protein producer
59 Item with a brim or crown

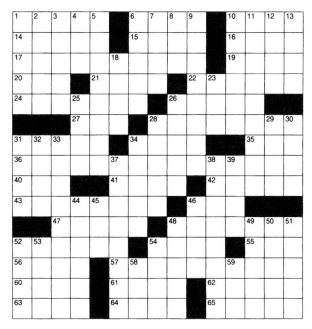

by Lynn Lempel

ACROSS

1 "Woe is me!"
5 With 72-Across, the end of 20-, 37-, 44- or 59-Across
10 Scribbles
14 Hiker's snack
15 Els of the links
16 Late Stuntmaster Knievel
17 Et ___ (and others)
18 Prices
19 Like a Playmate of the Month
20 1951 Montgomery Clift/Elizabeth Taylor film, with "A"
23 English county on the North Sea
24 Buckeyes' sch.
25 Place to wrestle
28 Kindergarten learning
32 Whinny
34 Missions, for short
37 Venus
40 Puppyish
42 Gullible
43 Suffix with cigar
44 Place to do business in the Old West
47 Use a Singer
48 Take ___ at (try)
49 Mlle., in Madrid
50 Luau souvenir
51 Goddess of the dawn
54 Lick of fire
59 1987 Prince song and album
64 Milliners' output
66 Scott who wrote "Presumed Innocent"
67 Dog that's a little of this, a little of that
68 Cotton swab
69 In unison
70 "That's clear"
71 Anatomical pouches
72 See 5-Across
73 "___ of the D'Urbervilles"

DOWN

1 Wide open, as the mouth
2 Lazes
3 Operatic solos
4 Cinnamon or cloves
5 Tenth: Prefix
6 Elvis's middle name
7 Part of M.I.T.: Abbr.
8 Many an art print, for short
9 Affirmatives
10 Bach's "___, Joy of Man's Desiring"
11 Hand protectors for bakers
12 It's between La. and N.M.
13 Using trickery
21 What a student crams for
22 Like lyrics
26 Playing marble
27 Passed
29 East Berlin's counterpart during the cold war
30 Rugged rock formation
31 Sounds in a barbershop
33 Opposite of WNW
34 In base eight
35 Total prize money
36 Earned run average, e.g.
38 Actor/composer Novello
39 Hatchling's site
41 Author LeShan
45 "___ to differ"
46 President before Wilson
52 Not in bottles, as beer
53 Man of many marches
55 Maximum or minimum
56 Make laugh
57 Doles (out)
58 ___ Park, Colo.
60 AOL and Road Runner: Abbr.
61 Too much: Fr.
62 Fine-tune
63 Still-life object
64 Mil. command bases
65 One ___ time

by Andrew Ries

ACROSS

1 It's rounded up in a roundup
5 Propel a bicycle
10 Pinnacle
14 Hawaii's "Valley Isle"
15 "___ Get Your Gun"
16 Linen fiber
17 Operation for a new liver or kidney
20 Home (in on)
21 Mao ___-tung
22 That woman
23 "The Sweetheart of Sigma ___"
26 Refuses to
28 Encourages
30 Jane who wrote "Sense and Sensibility"
32 Take home a trophy
34 Beer component
35 Swains
36 Cry after a bad swing
37 Decorates, as a cake
38 Beneficial substance in fruits, vegetables and tea
41 Feature of many a wedding dress
43 Picking ___ with
44 Alto or soprano
47 Letter-shaped building support
48 Small number
49 Yuletide songs
50 Mortarboard addition
52 Face-to-face test
54 Puppy's bite
55 Inventor Whitney
56 Grain in Cheerios
58 Great-great-great-great-great grand-father of Noah

60 Literary genre popular with women
66 Shortly
67 Message from a BlackBerry, maybe
68 Tiny critters found twice each in 17-, 38- and 60-Across
69 Impose, as a tax
70 Car dings
71 Yuletide

DOWN

1 Insurance grp.
2 Where a phone is held
3 Oriental ___
4 Actress Cameron
5 Sponsor
6 Company with a spectacular 2001 bankruptcy
7 Reproductive material
8 "___ it the truth!"
9 Made smaller
10 C.I.O.'s partner
11 Kind of suit
12 Street opening for a utility worker
13 Spreads
18 Most recent
19 Place to hang one's hat
23 Taxi
24 Shade
25 "I, Robot" author
27 Four
29 Key of Saint-Saëns's "Danse macabre"
31 Radio receiver parts
33 Eye part
36 ___ gras

39 Puffed up
40 King Arthur's burial place
41 Without metaphor
42 Mother-of-pearl source
45 151, in old Rome
46 Telepathy, e.g.
49 "Streets" of Venice
51 Period in history
53 Size again
57 It heals all wounds, in a saying
59 ___ Lee of Marvel Comics
61 One or more
62 Soup container
63 Year, in Spain
64 Sault ___ Marie
65 Fashion inits.

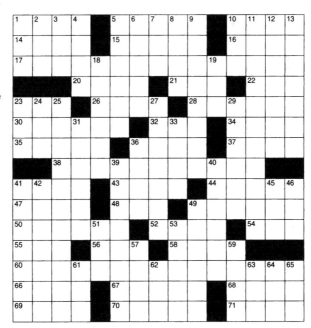

by Steven Ginzburg

ACROSS

1 Exercises sometimes done cross-legged
5 Basement's opposite
10 Place for a ship to come in
14 Rightmost bridge position
15 Grand Canyon transport
16 Western native
17 Base for turkey stuffing, often
19 Wagering parlors, for short
20 Madison Square Garden is one
21 On ___ (when challenged)
22 J. R. of "Dallas"
25 Leave furtively
28 Taoism founder
30 New Balance competitor
31 Opposed to
32 They're seen at marble tournaments
35 What the easiest path offers
41 Waiting to be mailed
42 "O.G. Original Gangster" rapper
43 Items in a "bank"
46 Off-course
48 Long-lasting housetop
51 Thrill
52 Appointed
53 Native of Tehran
55 "___ cost you!"
56 Sob stories
61 Orange throwaway
62 Miserable weather
63 Cash drawer
64 This, to Tomás
65 Pal
66 Cherry throwaway

DOWN

1 "Sure thing!"
2 Morsel for Dobbin
3 Overseer of govt. office bldgs.
4 Legendary sunken island
5 French cleric
6 Blinkers signal them
7 "My ___" (dinner host's offer)
8 Levin who wrote "Rosemary's Baby"
9 Fish-and-chips fish
10 Thingamajig
11 Canada's capital
12 Snake charmers' snakes
13 "One Flew Over the Cuckoo's Nest" author Ken
18 Work units
21 Preferred invitees
22 Carrier to Tel Aviv
23 Decrease gradually
24 Greek "I"
26 Have a home-cooked meal, say
27 "___ Fideles"
29 Salary recipient
33 Painting surface
34 Enzyme ending
36 Like a good-sounding piano
37 Emergency military transports
38 Annual hoops championship organizer, for short
39 Penny
40 Suffix with marion
43 Stack in a kitchen cabinet
44 "To be or not to be" speaker
45 Verdi opera
47 City near Lake Tahoe
48 Relative of the sandpiper
49 Lubricated
50 Emancipated
54 Regarding
56 "Naughty, naughty!"
57 "Float like a butterfly, sting like a bee" boxer
58 ___ and wisdom
59 Bullring shout
60 Shade tree

by Sarah Keller

ACROSS

1 Nightfall
5 Sonnet and sestina
10 The Beatles' "Back in the ___"
14 Korea's continent
15 Kind of ink
16 Artsy N.Y.C. locale
17 Many a Westminster show exhibitor
19 Aliens' craft, for short
20 Parrot
21 Makes a cartoon of
23 Robin or swallow
25 Swiss peak
26 Shepherd's domain
29 Mathematician John von ___
33 Play part
36 ___ Remus
38 Predestination
39 Cabbage salad
40 Features found in 17- and 64-Across and 11- and 28-Down
43 Hydrochloric ___
44 ___ noire
45 Sir or madam
46 The "r" in Aristotle
47 It is golden, it's said
49 Superlative ending
50 Louse-to-be
52 Ayatollah's predecessor
54 Walked unsteadily
59 "Lose Yourself" rapper
63 Sailor's greeting
64 Longtime Wal-Mart symbol
66 Grain grinder
67 Tarzan's transports
68 Fox TV's "American ___"

69 Gallup sampling
70 Shareholder's substitute
71 Beach composition

DOWN

1 Miami-___ County, Fla.
2 Quadrennial games org.
3 Sound of relief
4 Skewered lamb, e.g.
5 South Dakota's capital
6 Word before "ignition . . . liftoff!"
7 Icelandic epic
8 Demeanor
9 Wrap for Indira Gandhi
10 Everyday

11 Rear of the roof of the mouth
12 Home for an "old woman" in a nursery rhyme
13 Seamstress Betsy
18 Queens of France
22 Homo sapiens
24 Camper's bag
26 Kind of eclipse
27 Cain's eldest son
28 G.I. Joe, for one
30 Dull photo finish
31 Parthenon's home
32 Born: Fr.
34 Charges on a telephone bill
35 Little bird's sound
37 Ushered
39 Biol. or chem.

41 Geisha's sash
42 Like a sauna room
47 Jeanne d'Arc, e.g.: Abbr.
48 Shabby
51 Pastoral composition
53 Old 45 players
54 Wettish
55 Birthplace of seven U.S. presidents
56 Answer, as an invitation
57 Mideast potentate
58 T. Rex, e.g.
60 Zippo
61 Supply-and-demand subj.
62 Blend
65 Superman enemy ___ Luthor

by Edward M. Sessa

ACROSS

1 With 68-Across, bell ringer
5 Doing nothing
9 Speechify
14 Fashion designer Rabanne
15 Vehicle on tracks
16 Pugilist
17 No. on a bank statement
18 Grotto
19 Material for Elvis's blue shoes
20 Bell ringer
23 "California, ___ Come"
24 Spouse's meek agreement
28 See 52-Across
29 Cy Young Award winner Blue
33 Home that may have a live-in butler
34 Less certain
36 Archaeological site
37 Bell ringer
41 Go backpacking
42 Inside info for an investor, maybe
43 Sheep's cries
46 Unskilled laborer
47 Ordinal suffix
50 Kids' game involving an unwanted card
52 With 28-Across, winner of golf's 1997 U.S. Open
54 Bell ringer
58 Org.
61 Club that's not a wood
62 Al or Tipper
63 Book after Jonah
64 Emperor who reputedly fiddled while Rome burned
65 God of love

66 "Lord, ___?" (biblical query)
67 Pop music's Bee ___
68 See 1-Across

DOWN

1 Geronimo's tribe
2 Poet Lindsay
3 Happens
4 ___ Dame
5 Poison ivy symptom
6 Sketch
7 ___ lamp (1960s novelty)
8 Manicurist's item
9 Dwell (on)
10 Point A to point B and back
11 Firefighter's tool
12 Slugger Williams

13 "Able was I ___ I saw Elba"
21 Honda model
22 Joey with the Starliters
25 Waters, informally
26 Going ___ (fighting)
27 Stimpy's cartoon pal
30 Post-op spot, for short
31 One running away with a spoon, in a children's rhyme
32 Greek fabulist
34 Heartthrob
35 Baptism or bar mitzvah
37 Bit of medicine
38 Squeezed (out)
39 Palindromic tribe name

40 Forty-___ (gold rush participant)
41 "Curb Your Enthusiasm" airer
44 Chinese martial art
45 "___ 'em!"
47 "Bewitched" witch
48 Steering system component
49 Religious dissent
51 Faulkner's "As I Lay ___"
53 Star in Orion
55 Native Canadian
56 Stories passed down through generations
57 1961 space chimp
58 Pal in Paris
59 ___ boom bah
60 Lab field: Abbr.

by Sarah Keller

ACROSS

1 Put out, as a fire
6 Furry TV extraterrestrial
9 Arouse, as interest
14 "In my opinion . . ."
15 Place for sheep to graze
16 Mrs. Bush
17 Utensil used with flour
18 Perry Mason's field
19 Out of kilter
20 Old "Tonight Show" intro
23 Fork over
24 Word after show or know
25 Bygone Rambler mfr.
27 Classic arcade game
31 Set free
36 Pungent-smelling
37 Expensive tooth filling material
38 Sport with beefy grapplers
39 Admonition to a showboating athlete
42 Notes after do
43 Doll's cry
44 Almost any doo-wop tune
45 What a driver's license shows proof of
47 Makes tough
48 Understood
49 By way of
50 "Cheers" bartender
53 Kid's book with a hidden character
60 Atlantic or Pacific
62 Buddhist sect
63 Squirrel away
64 Suspect's story

65 Stephen of "The Crying Game"
66 Out of favor, informally
67 Derby prize
68 The whole shebang
69 Activities in 57-Down

DOWN

1 Satellite TV receiver
2 Garfield's pal, in the funnies
3 ___-friendly (simple to operate)
4 Put money in the bank
5 Poker player's headgear
6 Give the O.K.
7 Wife of Jacob

8 Young Bambi
9 Benchwarmer's plea
10 The Beatles' "___ the Walrus"
11 Wit's remark
12 Celestial bear
13 "Piece of cake!"
21 Rock's Bon Jovi
22 Nita of silent films
26 Windsor, notably
27 Father: Prefix
28 Felt sore
29 Oreo's filling
30 Sinking in mud
31 Hardly cramped
32 Director Kazan
33 Napped leather
34 Cybermessages
35 Stadium toppers

37 Pesky swarmer
40 Most common U.S. surname
41 Zero
46 Local noncollegian, to a collegian
47 Bro's sibling
49 Open to bribery
50 Suds maker
51 Rights org.
52 Golda of Israel
54 Poet Pound
55 Walk drunkenly
56 Top-rated
57 Features of science classes
58 "Dang!"
59 5:2, e.g., at a racetrack
61 Muscles to crunch

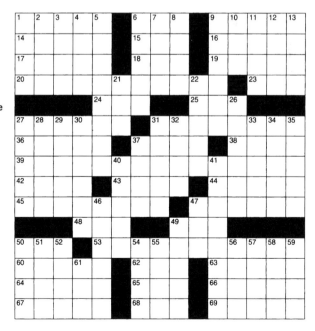

by Fred Piscop

ACROSS

1 Wager
4 Gush
10 Willie of the 1950s-'60s Giants
14 Israeli submachine gun
15 Last words of the Pledge of Allegiance
16 ___ vera
17 Atomic energy org.
18 *Popular Sunshine State vacation destination
20 Prepare to shoot
22 Docs
23 Stop for the night, as soldiers
25 Daughter's counterpart
26 Dartboard, for one
28 The "I" of I.M.F.: Abbr.
30 Austrian affirmatives
33 "The Thin Man" pooch
34 Rim
36 Put (down), as money
38 Theater focal point
40 Select, with "for"
41 Language akin to Urdu
42 Serious drinker
43 Arnaz of "I Love Lucy"
45 Depression-era migrant
46 "But I heard him exclaim, ___ he drove . . ."
47 Take too much of, briefly
49 Objected to
51 Brouhaha
52 Keep just below a boil
54 Not deceitful
58 Deck covering to keep out moisture

61 *Like players below the B team
63 "This means ___!"
64 Sets of points, in math
65 "Relax, soldier!"
66 U.K. record label
67 Newspaper essay
68 Mascara goes on them
69 King, in old Rome

DOWN

1 Part of a suicide squeeze
2 Poet Pound
3 *Material for an old-fashioned parade
4 Wipe off
5 Decorate with leaves
6 Erich who wrote "The Art of Loving"

7 Bygone Mideast inits.
8 Slender
9 Firstborn
10 "___ Whoopee!" (1920s hit)
11 One of the Baldwin brothers
12 Toy that might go "around the world"
13 Period in Cong.
19 Coach Rupp of college basketball
21 Take on
24 *Sties
26 One of the five senses
27 Fur trader John Jacob ___
29 Basketball rim attachments
30 Location for the ends of the answers to the four starred clues

31 Actress MacDowell
32 Schussed, e.g.
35 Dumbbell
37 Hampton of jazz fame
39 Wore away
44 Really, really big
48 ___ fin
50 Representations
51 Pungent-smelling
53 N.B.A. coach Thomas
54 Normandy town
55 Breakfast restaurant letters
56 "Good shot!"
57 Kett of old comics
59 Designate
60 Cereal whose ads feature a "silly rabbit"
62 ___ ipsa loquitur

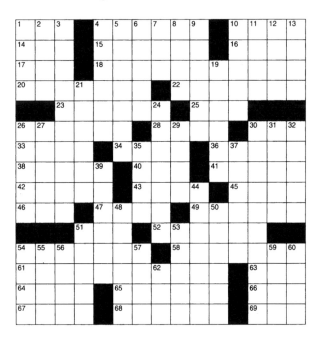

by Allan E. Parrish

ACROSS

1 Witty sorts
5 Make sense
10 Choice word
14 Think tank nugget
15 On the lam
16 Gerund, e.g.
17 Bond villain
19 Saw red?
20 Ph.D. thesis: Abbr.
21 Gets corroded
22 Bemoan
25 "Beats me" gesture
28 Rub out
29 Certain trout
33 Basis of a suit
34 Endless, poetically
35 Fraternity P
36 "Survivor" shelter
37 Some red wines
38 Obey the coxswain
39 Cheroot residue
40 Wings it
41 Place for
   a hoedown
42 Classic blues
   musician
44 Intuit
45 The "35" in
   John 11:35
46 Prodded
47 Woods or Irons
50 Flair
51 Laugh heartily
52 Patriarchal gorilla
58 Pond organism
59 Primp
60 Natural soother
61 Lounge in the sun
62 Feel nostalgia, e.g.
63 Crips or Bloods

DOWN

1 Faux 'fro?
2 Brouhaha
3 Goo in a do
4 Most mournful
5 Most-wanted
   group for a party
6 Puts on

7 Follow
   everywhere
8 Put to work
9 Part of r.p.m.
10 "Stop!"
11 Wall Street
   minimums
12 Fatty treat
   for birds
13 Pulls the
   plug on
18 Ticket cost?
21 Game sheet
22 Deadly
23 Work up
24 First first lady
25 Germ-free
26 As a result
   of this
27 Patronizes
   U-Haul, e.g.
29 Plays for time
30 Gofer's job

31 When repeated,
   cry by
   Shakespeare's
   Richard III
32 Consumed
   heartily
34 Octogenarian,
   for one
37 Pole tossed
   by Scots
41 Nontraditional
   chair style
43 Czech
   composer
   Antonín
44 Go up, up, up
46 Filmdom's Close
47 Omani, e.g.
48 Fast-food drink
49 Makes "it"
50 ". . . ___ after"
52 U-2 pilot, e.g.
53 Ill temper

54 Grazing ground
55 Carte start
56 Bamboozle
57 Fraternity
   party setup

by Steve Kahn

ACROSS

1 Indifferent to pleasure or pain
6 Close
10 Jacket
14 Toyota rival
15 Impulse
16 ___ of office
17 Taking back one's words in humiliation
19 "Oh, that's what you mean"
20 Excitement
21 ___-de-sac
22 Receiver of a legal transfer
24 Actress Zellweger
26 Anger
27 Negotiating in a no-nonsense way
32 Baby kangaroos
34 Joel who directed "Raising Arizona"
35 "These ___ the times that . . ."
36 One-named Art Deco designer
37 Vehicles in airplane aisles
39 "Love ___ the air"
40 Big elephant feature
41 Theater award
42 Prayers' ends
43 Pretending to be dead
47 The "et" of et cetera
48 Lock of hair
49 Rip off
53 Moo goo ___ pan
54 Ewe's call
57 Supervising
58 Raising a false alarm
61 Roman statesman ___ the Elder
62 Daylight saving, e.g.
63 ___ Rae (Sally Field title role)
64 Didn't just guess
65 Locales of mineral waters
66 Say with one's hand on the Bible

DOWN

1 New York stadium
2 Relative of a frog
3 Seeing through the deception of
4 Dictator Amin
5 Calls off
6 Cell centers
7 Misplay, e.g.
8 Slack-jawed
9 Edits
10 Neologist
11 Kiln
12 Suit to ___
13 Biblical pronoun
18 Sticky matter
23 Give ___ for one's money
24 Comedic actress Martha
25 Put into cipher
27 Four: Prefix
28 "___ Milk?"
29 Casey with a radio countdown
30 Land o' blarney
31 Achings
32 Army transport
33 Spoken
37 Leads, as an orchestra
38 "Hulk" director Lee
39 Don with a big mouth
41 One of the Sinatras
42 Hands out, as duties
44 Peter of Peter, Paul & Mary
45 Unrestrained revelries
46 Actor Penn
49 Marina fixture
50 "___ Almighty," 2007 film
51 Honor with a roast, say
52 What icicles do
54 Drill
55 ___ mater
56 Many miles away
59 Singer Sumac
60 "Man alive!"

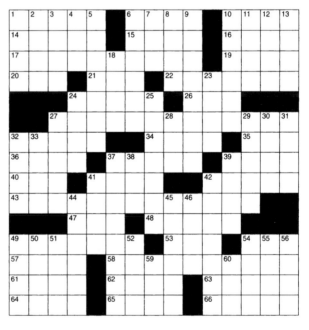

by Andrea Carla Michaels

ACROSS
1 Does sums
5 Pillow filler
9 Flapper hairdos
13 Scuttlebutt
14 Like a manly man
15 Escapade
16 Part of the eye that holds the iris
17 ___ and pains
18 What "thumbs up" means
19 Bandleader in the Polka Music Hall of Fame
22 Explosive initials
23 Pinocchio, famously
24 Mock
28 Dance with a wiggle
30 Lord
31 Card that's taken only by a trump
32 Mail carriers' assignments: Abbr.
34 Creamy soup
38 City where van Gogh painted sunflowers
40 Suffix with sucr- and lact-
41 Pacific republic
42 Substantial portion
45 Pile
46 Component of bronze
47 Permit
48 Washington's Capitol ___
50 Precipitates at about 32°F
52 Left hurriedly
54 New Deal program inits.
57 One who lost what's hidden in 19-, 34- and 42-Across
60 Hawaiian isle
63 More than perturbed
64 "Unfortunately . . ."
65 Give a hard time
66 Nobodies
67 Small field size
68 Branch of Islam
69 Plow pullers
70 Jean who wrote "Wide Sargasso Sea"

DOWN
1 No longer a minor
2 Couch
3 Made a stand and would go no further
4 Polaris, e.g.
5 Bangladesh's capital, old-style
6 Color of fall leaves
7 "Thank goodness!"
8 Rhinoplasty
9 Chap
10 Tree loved by squirrels
11 Maidenform product
12 Cloud's site
14 Psycho
20 90° turn
21 Ushered
25 "Fantastic Voyage" actress
26 Honda division
27 Get ready to drive, in golf
29 ___-friendly
30 Agents under J. Edgar Hoover, informally
32 Balsa transports
33 Path
35 Booty
36 Tempe sch.
37 Comedian Mort
39 1972 U.S./U.S.S.R. missile pact
43 Latin American with mixed ancestry
44 Oedipus' realm
49 Wedding vow
51 Doolittle of "My Fair Lady"
52 Distress signal shot into the air
53 Divulge
55 Explorer who proved that Greenland is an island
56 Basilica recesses
58 Fearsome dino
59 Jack of early late-night TV
60 ___ Butterworth's
61 What a doctor might ask you to say
62 Israeli gun

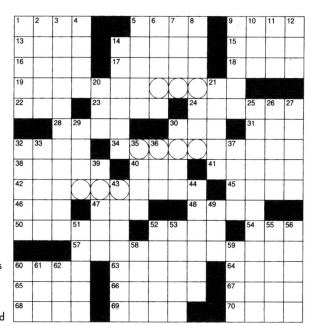

by Lynn Lempel

ACROSS

1 Started a cigarette
6 Sail supporter
10 Rooters
14 Left one's seat
15 Gumbo vegetable
16 Track shape
17 Allotment of heredity units?
19 Parks who pioneered in civil rights
20 Our language: Abbr.
21 Took the blue ribbon
22 Room to maneuver
24 Nuclear power apparatus
27 Top 10 tunes
28 Hole-punching tool
29 Slender cigar
33 Prefix with -hedron
36 Is false to the world
37 Get from ___ (progress slightly)
38 Battle of the ___ (men vs. women)
39 Stadium section
40 Studied primarily, at college
42 Holder of 88 keys
43 Caveman's era
44 Vintage automotive inits.
45 Tennis great Arthur
46 Mediums' meetings
50 Stewed to the gills
53 King Kong, e.g.
54 Lacto-___-vegetarian
55 Sitarist Shankar
56 Preacher's sky-high feeling?
60 Twistable cookie
61 Turn at roulette

62 Decaf brand
63 Give an alert
64 Direction of sunup
65 Sticky problem

DOWN

1 Hearty brew
2 Jim Carrey comedy "Me, Myself & ___"
3 Kingdom east of Fiji
4 Milk for all its worth
5 Pay-___-view
6 Travel by car
7 Closely related (to)
8 Sign at a sellout
9 Bikini wearers' markings

10 TV channel for golfers?
11 State frankly
12 Shuttle-launching org.
13 Murder
18 Delinquent G.I.
23 Greek H's
25 Pasta-and-potato-loving country?
26 Former rival of Pan Am
27 Safe place
29 Mischievous sprite
30 Director Kazan
31 Claim on property
32 Prefix with dynamic
33 Scots' caps
34 Coup d'___
35 Japanese P.M. during W.W. II

36 Mantel
38 Equine-looking fish
41 Take a siesta
42 Split ___ soup
44 Fishing line winder
46 Paid out
47 Nickels and dimes
48 Call to mind
49 Sunken ship finder
50 Furrowed part of the head
51 Dr. Zhivago's love
52 1964 Dave Clark Five song "Glad All ___"
53 Hertz rival
57 Mileage rating org.
58 Cleopatra's biter
59 Eastern "way"

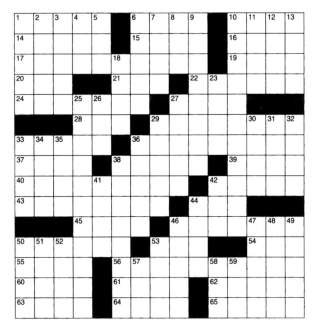

by Fred Piscop

ACROSS

1 "Lady Marmalade" singer ___ LaBelle
6 Musical phrase
10 On the briny
14 Birdlike
15 Poet ___ Khayyám
16 Butter slices
17 T. S. Eliot title character who measures out his life with coffee spoons
20 Not just recent
21 Muck
22 "The Simpsons" bartender
23 Light throw
26 Studio sign
29 Actress MacDowell of "Groundhog Day"
32 Really impressed
34 Geller with a spoon-bending act
35 Light golden lager
38 ___ Bator, Mongolia
39 Editor out to smear Spider-Man
42 Parti-colored
43 Dance class outfit
44 Quantity: Abbr.
45 Sheep cries
46 Rapids transits
50 A goose egg
52 Phobia
55 Unfortunate sound when you bend over
56 Hay storage locale
58 Saw-toothed
61 Vice president who once famously mashed "potato"
65 Come to shore
66 Baby bassoon?
67 War horse

68 Lyric poems
69 Puppy bites
70 Sexy nightwear

DOWN

1 ___ party (sleepover)
2 Frankie of "Beach Blanket Bingo"
3 Cultivated the soil
4 President who later served as chief justice
5 Initials on a cross
6 Where you might hear "Ride 'em, cowboy!"
7 Little devil
8 Distant
9 Lively '60s dance
10 Kitchen spill catcher
11 Brazil's largest city
12 And so on: Abbr.

13 "___ and ye shall receive"
18 CPR pro
19 Grocery offering
24 California city in a 1968 Dionne Warwick hit
25 Accumulation on the brow
27 Persia, today
28 ___ Tin Tin
30 Its first ad touted "1,000 songs in your pocket"
31 German article
33 Humorist Bombeck
36 Singsong syllables
37 Grain bundle
38 Beef quality graders: Abbr.
39 Guitarist Hendrix
40 747, e.g.
41 Be mistaken

42 La ___, Bolivia
45 Hit, as on the noggin
47 Worn at the edges
48 Like the Marquis de Sade or the Duke of Earl
49 Rapid
51 Unilever skin cream brand
53 Fireplace remnants
54 Necessary: Abbr.
57 Roger Rabbit or Donald Duck
59 Corrosion sign
60 Appraise
61 Female singer's 2001 album that debuted at #1
62 "Dear old" guy
63 Slugger's stat
64 Blouse or shirt

by Jeremy Horwitz

ACROSS

1 David or Victoria Beckham, e.g.
5 Bit of surveillance evidence
9 Muffin ingredient
13 When doubled, an old sitcom goodbye
14 Film format for domed theaters
15 Vibes
17 Derive (from)
18 Doofus
20 ___ flour
22 Sun. morning lecture
23 Novel on which "Clueless" is based
24 English philosopher who wrote "Wherever Law ends, Tyranny begins"
27 Doofus
29 Cheri
30 Parrot
31 Tablet
32 Part of U.S.P.S.
33 CD players
36 Stanley's love in "A Streetcar Named Desire"
38 Shown the door
40 Suffix with priest
41 Craggy mountain ridges
45 Computer command
46 Runaway bride or groom
47 Eyeliner problem
48 Doofus
51 Overweight plus
52 In awe
53 Airport stat.
54 Priestly vestment
55 Doofus
58 Catch sight of
62 RCA competitors
63 Wry Bombeck
64 AT&T's stylized globe, e.g.
65 Crave
66 Former Russian royalty
67 Pig and poi feast

DOWN

1 ___ and outs
2 Calico, e.g.
3 Sole
4 Doofus
5 Itsy-bitsy
6 Pierre's pal
7 Pretty violets
8 Sound bite, e.g.
9 "Pow!"
10 Media executive Murdoch
11 Scent
12 Mama Judd
16 Stretch of time
19 Difficult experiences
21 Opposite of 'neath
24 Expire
25 Cuts out
26 Nat and Natalie
27 Sis's sib
28 It's bound with twine
32 Many an ex-con
33 Recipient
34 Traitor
35 Kmart or Target
37 ___ land
39 Doofus
42 Nickname
43 Chicken ___
44 Work unit
46 Eastertime product
47 Pine-___
48 QB Marino and others
49 "Shall ___?" ("Want me to continue?")
50 Nary a soul
54 Hebrew month
56 Psychedelic drug
57 Doc's org.
59 Pittance
60 Organizer of one of four Grand Slam events: Abbr.
61 A person who is not a doofus

by C. W. Stewart

ACROSS

1 Private stash
6 Eighty-six
10 Very smart
14 Earthy pigment
15 Double-reed woodwind
16 Ruffian
17 Police ploys
20 Old Russian ruler
21 Lid trouble
22 Omar of TV's "House"
23 ___ of Man
25 Farm milk producers
27 Type
30 End-of-day spousal salutation
35 Clear, as a winter windshield
37 Crossed out
38 Sign of things to come
39 When said three times, a W.W. II movie
40 Give the giggles
42 Gallery showing works by Turner, Reynolds and Constable
43 Calendario units
44 Debussy's "La ___"
45 Lead down the aisle
46 "Call when you get the chance"
50 Flutter
51 Pocket particles
52 Sandbox item
54 Univ. lecturer
56 Way to go
58 Duchess of ___, Goya subject
62 Bogart/Hepburn film
65 Work in the garden
66 Use of a company car or private washroom, say
67 Took a shot at
68 Birds whose heads can rotate 135° left or right
69 "Got it"
70 Full of lip

DOWN

1 How much to pay
2 Play parts
3 Quickly growing "pet"
4 Painter Matisse
5 Wee bit of work
6 Best-seller list
7 Toe the line
8 What a welcome sight relieves
9 Neptune's realm
10 Lofted approaches to the green
11 Earring shape
12 Charged particles
13 They may be burned and boxed
18 1993 Israeli/Palestinian accords site
19 Swarm
24 "___ Drives Me Crazy," #1 hit by the Fine Young Cannibals
26 Like some smiles and loads
27 Holder of a dog's name and owner info
28 Téa of "Spanglish"
29 Russian ballet company
31 Outlying community
32 D-Day beach
33 Apportioned
34 First month in Madrid
36 Social workers' work
40 "You got that right!"
41 Pastries in "Sweeney Todd"
45 Action film firearm
47 Tick off
48 Mental grasp
49 Newswoman Paula
53 First lady after Hillary
54 "What a relief!"
55 Rod's partner
57 Decent plot
59 Island garlands
60 Theme of this puzzle
61 Pop artist Warhol
62 First and last digit in a Manhattan area code
63 Sch. in Troy, N.Y.
64 Parts of gals.

by Tom Heilman

ACROSS

1 Russian space station
4 "The Song of ___," old French epic
10 Spill the beans
14 Half of dos
15 Blackboard appurtenance
16 Like hands after eating potato chips
17 It's worth listening to
19 Info in a used car ad
20 Toll
21 Conduct a survey
23 Republic from which Montenegro gained its independence
25 ___-jongg
26 Sherlock Holmes portrayer
33 Nabokov heroine
35 "Don't ___ on me" (slogan of the American Revolution)
36 Where San Diego is: Abbr.
37 Art ___
39 Expensive coat
41 Cravings
42 Not silently
44 Laughing
46 Drivers' org.
47 Perfect shape
50 Building wing
51 Sale markdown indicator
54 Variety of rose
60 Decorative sofa fabric
61 River of Switzerland
62 Where the first words of 17-, 26- and 47-Across may be found
64 It may be in the doghouse
65 Its alphabet starts with alif
66 Bard's "before"
67 Hightail it
68 Tennessee team
69 "Help!"

DOWN

1 Scents used for perfume
2 Senseless
3 English philosopher called "Doctor Mirabilis"
4 One who sees it like it is
5 Fort ___, former Army post on Monterey Bay
6 Source of basalt
7 Purchase stipulation
8 Place for a crick
9 Imagined
10 Cry of glee
11 Stead
12 Chester Arthur's middle name
13 Polar explorer Richard
18 Isle of exile
22 Sis-boom-bahs
24 Snobs put them on
27 Memorize, as lines
28 Raging mad
29 He lost to Dwight
30 They're controlled by the moon
31 "Peter Pan" dog
32 Actress Lanchester, who married Charles Laughton
33 "Madam, I'm ___"
34 Place to get a Reuben
38 Catcher of sound waves
40 ___'acte
43 Mid seventh-century date
45 Haberdashery items: Var.
48 Dated
49 Smell
52 Old Oldsmobile
53 They may be dominant
54 Knife handle
55 Where Bill and Hillary met
56 La ___ Tar Pits
57 Hatcher or Garr
58 Part of Q.E.D.
59 "I Do, I Do, I Do, I Do, I Do" group
63 Winning cry in a card game

by Linda Schechet Tucker

ACROSS

1 Trots
5 Seaweed product
9 Visual movement popularized in the 1960s
14 Twist-apart treat
15 God, for George Burn or Morgan Freeman
16 U.P.S. supply
17 One . . .
20 Artist's mishap
21 79, for gold: Abbr.
22 Brenner Pass locale
23 Many a TV clip
25 "i" completer
27 Helpless?
30 Headed out
32 Averse
36 Noted polonaise composer
38 Kind of vaccine
40 Horse course
41 Two . . .
44 Prefix with con
45 W.W. I German admiral
46 Rafael's wrap
47 On edge
49 Big atlas section
51 Fateful March date
52 Mother's hermana
54 Cable for money?
56 Iolani Palace locale
59 Simmer (down)
61 "I wanna!"
65 Three . . .
68 End of a fight
69 Langston Hughes poem
70 Largest volcano in Europe
71 Athenian lawgiver who introduced trial by jury
72 Big do
73 "Durn it!"

DOWN

1 Writes quickly
2 City near Provo
3 Subject of modern "mapping"
4 Fizzy drinks at a five-and-ten
5 J.F.K. posting: Abbr.
6 Start limping
7 One, two and three . . . or this puzzle's title
8 Guide strap
9 Baby docs, briefly
10 It has eyes that can't see
11 1½ rotation leap
12 Bring in the sheaves
13 Tut's kin?
18 Goof
19 O.K. sign
24 Confess (to)
26 Half an old comedy duo
27 Bloodhound's trail
28 "Golly"
29 Access the Web
31 "Don't give up!"
33 In first place
34 Brownish gray
35 Ballyhoos
37 Immigrant from Japan
39 Analyze, as ore
42 Grant-giving org.
43 High school course, for short
48 Wall plaster
50 "Yes, you are!" retort
53 Crackerjack
55 Mom's skill, briefly
56 Makes up one's mind (to)
57 Sleek, in auto talk
58 Burglar's booty
60 "You wish!"
62 Prefix with physical
63 Thomas who wrote "The Magic Mountain"
64 Slate, e.g., for short
66 Rooster's mate
67 It goes for a buck

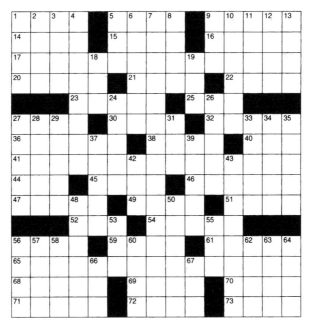

by Manny Nosowsky

18 TUESDAY

ACROSS

1 The whole ball of wax
5 Court cry
9 Last budget category, usually: Abbr.
13 Loafer, for one
14 Fabricate
15 Mediterranean island country
16 Golf club used in a bunker
18 Bird-related
19 USAir rival
20 Like Methuselah
21 Invent
22 Butcher's device
25 Examine
29 Pizazz
30 At full speed
31 Xerox machine output
36 Architect Ludwig Mies van der ___
37 Krispy ___ Doughnuts
38 Nabisco cookie
39 Tourist shop purchases
41 Avoid, as work
42 N.Y.C. cultural institution
43 Taste bud locale
44 U.S.S. Nautilus, for one
49 Show to be false
50 Computer file name extension
51 Haw's partner
54 Sierra ___
55 Spider-Man or the Green Lantern
58 Religion of the Koran
59 Like the Sahara
60 Singer Fitzgerald
61 Cop's path
62 "Toodles," in Milan
63 Marvel Comics mutants

DOWN

1 Secretary: Abbr.
2 Microwave option
3 Mrs. Chaplin
4 1-Across's end, in England
5 Frittata, e.g.
6 When said three times, et cetera
7 Heart chart, for short
8 New York's Tappan ___ Bridge
9 Expert
10 Troy story?
11 Union member
12 Chair person?
15 Name after Dan or San
17 "Pretty ___" (Richard Gere/Julia Roberts movie)
21 Shipping container
23 Iran's capital
24 ___ on to (grabs)
25 Swedish version of Lawrence
26 Melville novel
27 Waikiki Beach locale
28 Ukraine's capital
31 ___ ballerina
32 Big band saxophonist Al
33 Not a reproduction: Abbr.
34 The Pan-American Highway runs through it
35 Oxen holder
37 Séance sound
40 Rapper Marshall Mathers, familiarly
41 On the wagon
43 Some supper club attire
44 Improvise
45 Reagan cabinet member
46 Deadly virus
47 Charge
48 Brownish photo tint
51 Captain's position
52 Writer ___ Stanley Gardner
53 Séance sound
55 Pouch
56 "Psychic" Geller
57 Voodoo doctor's doing

by Christina Houlihan Kelly

ACROSS

1 Inane
5 ___ scan (biometric authentication method)
9 Districted
14 Cynic's comment
15 Payload delivery org.
16 Beam
17 Helpful person's line
20 Spiral in space
21 Most comfy
22 Jazz dance
23 Vice squad arrestees, perhaps
25 Perturbation
27 Autumn bloomer
32 With 42-Across, helpful person's line
37 Mesa tribe
38 Philosophy of bare existence?
39 Log-in info
41 Writer Waugh
42 See 32-Across
46 Like good pianos and engines
48 Levitated
49 Versatile fabric
51 Lives on
56 Spode ensembles
60 Coterie
61 Helpful person's line
64 Popular place for 18-Down
65 Tied up
66 Reel in
67 With cunning
68 St. Andrew's Day observer
69 Virtual mart

DOWN

1 Small jobs for a body shop
2 Kriegsmarine vessel
3 ___ Park (noted lab site)
4 Substitute players
5 Annual racing classic
6 Squealer
7 Prefix with tonic
8 "Hello, Dolly!" jazzman
9 One of the Gabors
10 Bygone Dodge
11 Giant in footwear
12 Graceful shaders
13 It's repellent
18 Sojourners abroad, for short
19 Darlin'
23 Elbow
24 Prospecting find
26 1989's ___ Prieta earthquake
28 Flushing stadium
29 Having a hard time deciding
30 Like "Paradise Lost"
31 Ferris wheel or bumper cars
32 Swarm member
33 "To Sir With Love" singer, 1967
34 Mideast harbor city
35 Cubes at Harrah's
36 Bother
40 ___ Artois beer
43 Agrees
44 Sellout letters
45 Lithium-___ battery
47 Stylish
50 Dough producer, briefly
52 Airplane seating request
53 Fowl entree
54 ___ deaf ear to
55 Not yet gentrified
56 Much of a waitress's income
57 And others, for short
58 Cockeyed
59 Clipper's sheet
60 ¢
62 Piping compound, briefly
63 Fierce type, astrologically

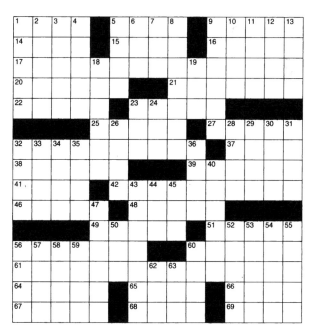

by Chuck Deodene

ACROSS

1 ___ Bartlet, president on "The West Wing"
4 John of "Full House"
10 Voodoo charm
14 Org. that publishes health studies
15 Butt in
16 One who may be caught off base?
17 Food transportation . . . that Harry Belafonte sang about
19 Place for a footballer's pad
20 Indiana and Ohio State are in it
21 Play ice hockey
23 Charles Lamb, pseudonymously
24 . . . that's an ambulance, in slang
28 It ends in the fall: Abbr.
29 Shade of green
31 Helpful
32 Symbol of love
36 "Sometimes you feel like ___"
37 . . . that a rube might fall off
39 Al Jazeera viewer, typically
41 He danced in "Silk Stockings"
42 Put on the payroll
44 Stimpy's cartoon pal
45 Org. for drivers?
48 . . . that may be upset
52 Place to load and unload
53 R & B singer Mary J. ___
54 Sen. Feinstein
56 Pork chop?
59 . . . that's a source of easy money

61 Declare
62 Cliff hangers?
63 Some like it hot
64 Word with telephoto or zoom
65 San Fernando Valley district
66 Doofus

DOWN

1 Poked
2 Communicates with online
3 "Phooey!"
4 Trig function
5 Tax cheat chaser, informally
6 Alert for a fleeing prisoner, in brief
7 Bullwinkle, e.g.
8 Japanese city whose name means "large hill"

9 Go after
10 Stick out one's tongue, maybe
11 Hold title to
12 Coffee, slangily
13 Corrida cheer
18 One ___ time
22 Afternoon hour
24 Home run hero of '61
25 Icky stuff
26 Home of the Cowboys: Abbr.
27 New Jersey cager
29 Part of r.p.m.
30 Novelist Ferber
32 Mingle (with)
33 Make a choice
34 Crank up
35 Keystone State port
37 Rain delay roll-out

38 Caterer's coffee holder
39 "So it's you!"
40 Boot Hill letters
43 Actor Benicio ___ Toro
45 Party animal?
46 Wish offerers
47 Soccer venues
49 Prop for Groucho Marx
50 See eye to eye
51 Plays parent to
52 72, at Augusta
54 Turned blue, maybe
55 "___ deal!"
56 Kilmer who once played Batman
57 She raised Cain
58 Bridge capacity unit
60 Compete

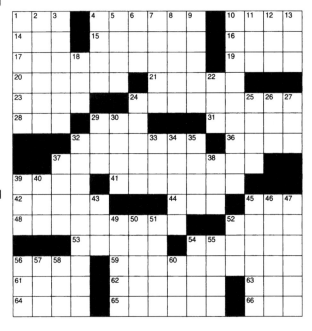

by Randall J. Hartman

ACROSS

1 "Do you like green eggs and ham?" speaker
7 In the style of
10 Lao-tzu's way
13 Meeting handout
14 Broke from the band, maybe
17 Cosmopolitan staple
19 Date
20 Uncertainties
21 It can be silly
22 Spot en el mar
24 W.W. I German admiral
26 N.F.L. star
32 Slip
33 Conquistador's quest
34 Actress Turner
36 Opposite of WSW
37 Period of human benightedness
41 Stroke
42 Overall feel
44 Coquettish
45 Relative of a mole
47 Colorful bed cover
51 Corrida cheers
52 Pageant adornment
53 Highest peak of Crete
56 Egg: Prefix
57 Wide shoe spec
60 "Behave!" . . . and a hint to this puzzle's theme
65 Representative
66 Tie, as a score
67 Cry between "ready" and "go!"
68 "Kid-tested" breakfast cereal
69 Keep

DOWN

1 Fools
2 Author James
3 Slight
4 Special connections
5 Bustle
6 Port seized by Adm. Dewey, 1898
7 Poking tools
8 Luau offering
9 Queen of the hill?
10 Ballyhoo
11 Dismounted
12 Like mud
15 Easygoing
16 Sound at a greased pig contest
18 In the distance
22 Figs. clustered around 100
23 Like a malfeasant, often
24 Fluids in bags
25 Bull Moose party: Abbr.
26 Appeal
27 Incurred, as charges
28 "La Traviata," e.g.
29 Site of the first Asian Olympics
30 Kind of pants
31 Prepare to propose
35 1, for hydrogen: Abbr.
38 What a massage may ease
39 Theater seating
40 Titles for attys.
43 In disagreement
46 "Say what?"
48 Pottery materials
49 Reply, briefly
50 Onetime German leader
53 Mlles. after marriage
54 Red-bordered magazine
55 The "W" in Geo. W. Bush, e.g.
56 Straight-horned African animal
57 Author Ferber
58 Prefix with distant
59 "SportsCenter" channel
61 Yellow ribbon holder, in song
62 Geller with a psychic act
63 St. crosser
64 Bring home

by Oliver Hill

ACROSS

1 Speaks, informally
4 Speak
9 Smokey Robinson's music genre, for short
14 ___ de France
15 End of a hangman's rope
16 Love to bits
17 BORE
20 Have ___ in one's head
21 ___ and outs
22 The "I" in T.G.I.F.
23 BOAR
28 Nap
29 "Golden" song
32 Ad-lib, musically
35 Sign before Virgo
36 Person performing an exorcism
37 Gives a stage cue
40 Honeybunch or cutie pie
41 Glowing remnants of a fire
42 Abbr. after many a general's name
43 Meyerbeer's "___ Huguenots"
44 Painting surface
45 Publisher of Cosmopolitan and Good Housekeeping
48 BOER
53 Before, in poetry
55 Baseballer Mel
56 "Maria ___," Jimmy Dorsey #1 hit
57 BOHR
62 Actress Garbo
63 "Er . . . um . . ."
64 Old tennis racket string material
65 Stand for a portrait

66 Taboos
67 Cry before "Get your hands off!"

DOWN

1 Have a chair by, as a table
2 ___ Yale, for whom Yale University is named
3 Six in 1,000,000
4 Out of sight
5 Also
6 ___ Sawyer
7 Reverse of WNW
8 Fix the electrical connections of
9 Didn't have enough supplies
10 Problem in focusing, for short
11 "Don't worry about it"
12 "Phooey!"
13 Panhandles
18 Club with a lodge
19 Bankbook abbr.
24 Knuckleheads
25 Tribulations
26 ___ dye
27 Lena or Ken of film
30 "This ___ . . . Then" (Jennifer Lopez album)
31 French summers
32 Computer image file format
33 French weapon
34 Sights at after-Christmas sales

36 Lab's ___ dish
38 Mini-plateau
39 "Will you marry me?," e.g.
40 Brandy fruit
42 Hoops official
45 Sticker through a lady's headgear
46 Coils of yarn
47 Soft powder
49 Biblical suffix
50 Stable sound
51 Come afterward
52 Wretched
53 Scoring advantage
54 ___ avis
58 Suffix with Israel
59 Dr. provider
60 Japanese moolah
61 ___ Paulo, Brazil

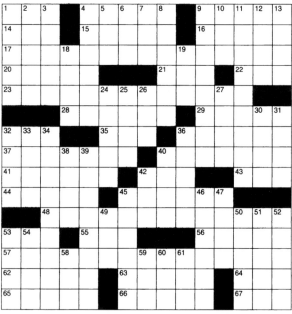

by Timothy Powell

ACROSS

1 Show anger
5 Round before the final
9 Washroom tub
14 Ph.D. awarder
15 Gave the boot
16 Blessing-inducing sound
17 Flank
18 Gimlet garnish
19 Crockpot concoctions
20 Relax during a drill
23 Temp's work unit
24 Polite affirmation
25 Brazilian dance
27 Big Apple awards
30 Like hair, usually, after combing
33 Post-O.R. stop
36 Craps natural
38 Impoverished
39 Sgt. Friday's org.
41 Calendar units hidden in 20- and 61-Across and 11-and 35-Down
43 Worker's pay
44 Like a brainiac
46 Fire remnants
48 The "R" in Roy G. Biv
49 Trojan War hero
51 Popular snack chip
53 Surveyor Jeremiah, for whom a famous line is partly named
55 Beatle, endearingly
59 Meadow sound
61 Sunshine State school
64 Minute Maid Park player
66 Baylor's city
67 Sp. girl
68 Rodeo animal
69 From the top
70 Ticks off
71 TV shout-out from the team bench
72 It's sold in skeins
73 "Great" kid-lit detective

DOWN

1 Hard to please
2 Bring together
3 Greedy monarch
4 "Nevertheless . . ."
5 On the payroll
6 Lighted sign in a theater
7 Hand-waver's cry
8 They may be bright
9 One in the infield
10 Follow direction?
11 Show sadness
12 Political caucus state
13 Like a yenta
21 "That's mine!"
22 Deplete, as energy
26 Cold one
28 FEMA recommendation, briefly
29 Play by a different ___ rules
31 Upper hand
32 Like batik fabrics
33 Ingrid's role in "Casablanca"
34 Showed up
35 "Time to rise, sleepyhead!"
37 Within earshot
40 Zwei follower
42 Lose the spare tire
45 Schedule B or C, e.g.
47 Ancient Greek colonnade
50 La preceder
52 Chooses to participate
54 "Impossible!"
56 ___ firma
57 Largish combo
58 Terrible twos, e.g.
59 Bad-mouth
60 Sparkling wine city
62 ___ deficit (lost money)
63 Pastry prettifier
65 Vintage auto

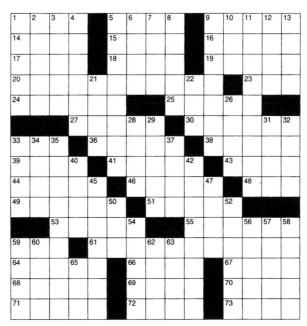

by Michael Kaplan

ACROSS
1 Play place
6 Ballroom dance
11 Chart-topper
14 Sign of spring
15 Mountaineer's tool
16 ET's ride
17 Play follower, usually
19 Unruly do
20 Amateurish
21 "___ economy is always beauty": Henry James
23 Buggy rider
26 Loofah, e.g.
30 108-card game
31 Start the pot
32 Pest control brand
33 Spoil
35 Bibliophile's suffix
36 Tipplers
37 Circulatory system flow
41 Singer ___ P. Morgan
43 Early 11th-century year
44 Back at sea?
47 Actress Chase of "Now, Voyager"
48 For dieters
51 Smidgen
52 Shoot-'em-up figure
54 Harmony, briefly
55 Clobber, biblically
56 Computer that uses OS X
58 Director Lee
59 What the starts of 17-, 26-, 37- and 52-Across are
66 Crib cry
67 Burger topper, maybe
68 Site of Ali's Rumble in the Jungle
69 Salon job
70 Cuts and pastes
71 TV awards

DOWN
1 Amniotic ___
2 Play about Capote
3 Put on TV
4 Manage, barely
5 Jacob's twin
6 G.I.'s helmet, slangily
7 Duke's sports org.
8 "Read Across America" grp.
9 Guy's partner
10 Primrose family member
11 Saroyan novel, with "The"
12 "It slipped my mind!"
13 Letterman lists
18 ID on a dust jacket
22 Acknowledges nonverbally
23 PC glitch
24 "Wheel of Fortune" buy
25 Hoops coach with the most N.C.A.A. Division I wins
27 Playful mockery
28 Rural event on horseback
29 Work out in the ring
31 Commotion
34 Red Sox div.
38 Old Dodge
39 Singer of the 1962 hit "The Wanderer"
40 Guinness Book suffix
41 Tools for making twisty cuts
42 Barnard grads
45 Bled, like dyes
46 "Deal or No Deal" network
49 Fakes, as an injury
50 Weaponry
53 Leave alone
54 "Beat it!"
57 Wood-shaping tool
60 Suffered from
61 Here, in Paris
62 "I'm kidding!"
63 Deadeye's asset
64 Dryly amusing
65 Nintendo's Super ___

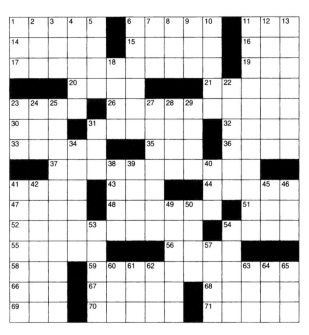

by Alan Arbesfeld

ACROSS

1 Peak
5 Chattered incessantly
10 TV horse introduced in 1955 . . . or a Plymouth model introduced in 1956
14 Partiality
15 Seeing red
16 Prime draft status
17 Drug-yielding plant
18 Opposite of serenity
19 Cartoonist Al
20 Scary sound from the ocean?
23 Park, e.g., in N.Y.C.
25 "Sting like a bee" athlete
26 Having seniority
28 Scary sound from a war zone?
33 Juillet's season
34 Kodiak native
35 Physics unit
36 Theory's start
37 Scary sound from a cornfield?
41 Splinter group
44 Motel-discount grp.
45 Sales slips: Abbr.
49 Galley implement
50 Scary sound from a steeple?
53 Tedious
55 Boot part
56 "Whew!"
57 Misspells, say, as a ghost might at 20-, 28-, 37- and 50-Across?
62 Abominate
63 African antelope
64 Hot rod's rod
67 ___ Lackawanna Railroad
68 Countryish
69 Boot part
70 Card game for three
71 Walk leisurely
72 Stealth bomber org.

DOWN

1 Charles Gibson's network
2 A.F.L.-___
3 Cane cutter
4 Biblical son who sold his birthright
5 Wavelet
6 Language whose alphabet starts alif, ba, ta, tha . . .
7 Child's caretaker
8 Suffix with hypn-
9 Part of a bottle or a guitar
10 Kind of point
11 Helpless?
12 Filled to the gills
13 Big fat mouth
21 Country just south of Sicily
22 Moo goo gai pan pan
23 Lawyers' org.
24 Kilmer of "The Doors"
27 ___ Irvin, classic artist for The New Yorker
29 Cowlick, e.g.
30 Fit for a king
31 Blunder
32 "Long ___ and far away . . ."
36 Creep (along)
38 Name that's an anagram of 27-Down
39 ___ de mer
40 Egyptian dry measure equal to about five-and-a-half bushels
41 Soak (up)
42 Tag for a particular purpose
43 Neighbor of Slovenia
46 Co. addresses, often
47 A duo
48 Crafty
50 Tournament pass
51 Like some music
52 Musically improvise
54 Sport utilizing a clay disk
58 Hospital shipments
59 Styptic agent
60 Part of a fishhook
61 Island with Waimea Bay
62 Gentlemen
65 Meadow
66 Shoemaker's helper, in a fairy tale

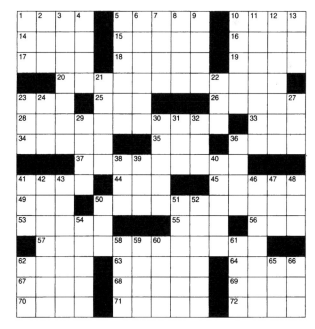

by Gary Steinmehl

ACROSS

1 Home in an old warehouse district
5 Virus named for a river
10 Trans-Siberian Railroad stop
14 Peculiar: Prefix
15 U.S./Canada early warning syst.
16 City bond, for short
17 Eisenhower was one
20 Move unsteadily
21 Delon of "Purple Noon"
22 Cedar Rapids college
23 2:30, aboard ship
27 Dele undoers
29 Something new
30 Ho Chi Minh's capital
31 Boris Godunov, for one
32 Rove, with "about"
35 Full range
37 It's off the tip of Italy
40 Bad-mouth
41 ___ war syndrome
45 ___ plume
46 Chiang Kai-shek's capital
48 Mountain cats
49 Rests for a bit
52 Singleton
53 "Waiting for Lefty" playwright
54 Like Dickens's Dodger
57 Shortly after quitting time, for many
62 Forearm bone
63 Shul V.I.P.
64 Pizzeria fixture
65 Hot times in France
66 Befuddled
67 Try for a role

DOWN

1 Brit's elevator
2 Garfield's foil
3 Nickel
4 Slugging it out
5 ___'acte
6 Feathery wrap
7 Bobby of the Bruins
8 Dillydally
9 Fruity quencher
10 Brunch dish
11 Wall art
12 Symbol of slowness
13 Ceramists' baking chambers
18 Welcomes, as a guest at one's home
19 Catches red-handed
23 Jack Sprat's taboo
24 Hypotheticals
25 Rome's ___ Veneto
26 Blunders
27 Outbuilding
28 Vehicle with a medallion
32 Request for a congratulatory slap
33 Pierce player
34 Gray concealers
36 End-of-workweek cry
38 At a cruise stop
39 Be worth
42 AP competitor
43 "My Name Is Asher ___"
44 "For shame!"
46 Colorful fishes
47 Helper: Abbr.
49 Brimless cap
50 At least 21
51 "The Family Circus" cartoonist Bil
54 Home to most Turks
55 Iris's place
56 Libraries do it
58 Big Band ___
59 Turn state's evidence
60 "Sesame Street" network
61 Honest ___

by John Underwood

ACROSS

1 Did one leg of an Ironman competition
5 Mike holder on a film set
9 Luxuriant fur
14 Wheeling's river
15 Castaway's spot
16 Ballerinas' skirts
17 Queen of Carthage who loved Aeneas
18 Part of a blind
19 Paradises
20 Start of a newspaper headline about a workplace mishap
23 HBO competitor
24 U.N. workers' grp.
25 Mil. decoration
28 Special ___
30 Not subtle at all
34 Headline, part 2
37 Mideast ruler: Var.
38 Ingenuous
39 Flight info, for short
40 Subject for a chiropractor
41 Feudal serf
42 Headline, part 3
44 Stung
46 I, in old Rome
47 C.I.A. predecessor
48 ___ Lanka
49 Something that may be drawn in a fight
51 End of the headline
59 Soothing plants
60 Shook, maybe
61 Panache
63 Map detail
64 Beige
65 Muse of history
66 Blacksmiths' tools
67 Bubble source
68 Soviet news agency

DOWN

1 Greenskeeper's supply
2 Caprice
3 "Celeste ___" (aria)
4 Gazes dreamily
5 Knights' neighbors
6 1952 Winter Olympics site
7 Minnesota's St. ___ College
8 Hand (out)
9 Designer McCartney, daughter of Paul and Linda
10 Sound recording
11 Bingo call
12 Broadway's ___- Fontanne Theater
13 Brand name that's coincidentally Italian for "it"
21 Alternative to 1% or 2%
22 Easter decoration
25 Beach sights
26 Twitch
27 Great Wall site
29 Lieu
30 Astronomer Tycho ___
31 Protein acid, for short
32 Boys, in Bogotá
33 Close-fitting tartan pants
35 Ignore the alarm?
36 List ender
40 [How boring!]
42 Rabin's predecessor
43 "Go ahead, tell me"
45 No-tell motel happenings
50 Construct
51 Evenhanded
52 It's hinged with the humerus
53 Red ink entry
54 Meadow mamas
55 Fashion's Chanel
56 Gumbo ingredient
57 "___ Enchanted" (Gail Carson Levine book)
58 Place for a seat of honor
62 Dissenting chorus

by Ray Fontenot

ACROSS

1 Lovers' scrap
5 Nanki-Poo's father
11 Cabinet dept.
14 Samovars
15 Artillery unit member
16 Some eggs
17 McGarrett's TV catchphrase
19 Unit of RAM
20 Father figure?
21 By way of
22 600-homer club member
23 Alights
24 Question for a hitchhiker
26 Giant in Cooperstown
27 Eggs, in labs
29 Biblical landing spot
30 Putting a toe in the water, say
32 Hockey position
35 Paris Métro station next to a music center
36 Shout from the phone
39 Resident of Medina
42 ___' Pea
43 Type size
47 Cause of odd weather
49 Wrap up
51 ___ de plume
52 Chevy truck slogan, once
55 John of London
57 Ward (off)
58 Sellout sign
59 World Cup chant
60 Italian diminutive suffix
61 Singles bar repertoire (and a hint to 17-, 24-, 36- and 52-Across)
63 Make darts, say
64 Cry after "Psst!"
65 For fear that
66 Farm brooder
67 Casually add
68 Pseudocultured

DOWN

1 Side story
2 Apportion, as costs
3 Rubs oil on
4 Clicked one's tongue
5 Ones minding the store: Abbr.
6 Birth control option, briefly
7 Scalawag
8 ___ Hall, Diane Keaton role
9 "Gracias" response
10 Cortés's prize
11 Tall wardrobe
12 Succeeds in a big way
13 Yachting event
18 "Happy Motoring" brand
22 Top-notch, to a Brit
24 Innocents
25 Suffix with buck
28 Bugs on a highway
31 Straightened (up)
33 "___ what?"
34 Rosetta stone language
37 Yothers of "Family Ties"
38 Kobe cash
39 Me-first
40 Property recipient, in law
41 Hardly a celebrity
44 Chanter
45 Least ruffled
46 General pardon
48 "Twelfth Night" lover
50 Secluded valley
53 Violists' places: Abbr.
54 Burger go-withs
56 Hyams of 1920s–'30s films
59 Shop window sign
61 Word with boss or bull
62 New England state sch.

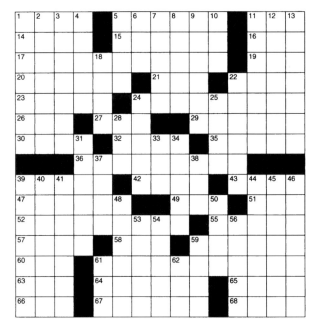

by Patrick Blindauer

ACROSS

1 Steering wheel option
5 Superior to
10 Pacific island nation
14 Gas leak evidence
15 20 Mule Team compound
16 Canadian dollar bird
17 Nativity trio
18 Ain't grammatical?
19 Wilson of "Zoolander"
20 Expresses scorn
22 Means' partner
23 Swiss artist Paul
24 Early TV comic Louis
26 Blowhard's speech
29 1966 Rolling Stones hit
34 Give a keynote
35 Eco-friendly
36 Author Fleming
37 Hose woes
38 Nymph of Greek myth
39 ___ breve
40 Upper-left key
41 Prison-related
42 Prefix with task
43 Scan
45 Start a new hand
46 Part of H.R.H.
47 Tubular pasta
48 Place to dock
51 Human hand characteristic
57 In good shape
58 Rhone feeder
59 Back muscles, for short
60 Loafing

61 Word before tube or self
62 Neutral shade
63 Face, slangily
64 They may be the pits
65 Percolate

DOWN

1 Barnum midget
2 Actress Lupino and others
3 Business card graphic
4 Tchotchkes
5 Brought down
6 Held up
7 Creme-filled snack
8 U-Haul rentals
9 Like some warranties
10 Lapel insert

11 Corn Belt state
12 "Friends" spinoff
13 Roadside stops
21 Gen. Robert ___
25 Nikkei average currency
26 It may stick out
27 Pie part
28 Dressing choice
29 Dickens's ___ Heep
30 Boortz of talk radio
31 ___ Lacs, Minn.
32 Big Three meeting place
33 Kind of sketch
35 What a prisoner's tattoo may signify
38 Anxiety may be a symptom of it

39 Quarterbacks' play changes
41 Rue Morgue's creator
42 Prefix with physics
44 Rappers' skill
45 Stair parts
47 Stopped listening, with "out"
48 Swab name
49 Pakistani tongue
50 Has a fever, say
52 Plexiglas unit
53 Corn bread
54 Queen Anne's ___
55 To be, in France
56 Encouraging sign

by Jayne and Alex Boisvert

ACROSS

1 It may be held together by twine
5 Bit of broccoli
10 Tussle
15 ___ Turing, the Father of Computer Science
16 Usher's domain
17 Incinerator deposit
18 Do a post office job
19 Prenatal
20 It leaves the left ventricle
21 Start of an idle question
24 Long look
25 Canasta plays
26 Kon-Tiki Museum site
30 Mid sixth-century year
31 ___-cow
34 Robbie Knievel's father
38 Blow a mean horn
40 Ruby's victim
42 Middle of the question
45 Book before Jeremiah
46 Drink with tempura
47 Antelope's playmate
48 Inc., in St. Ives
49 Insolence
51 Rover's pal
53 Low-fat breakfast dish
55 Cambria, today
60 End of the question
66 Tenth of a decathlon
67 Manhattan Project result
68 Contact at a hospital, say
69 Pad paper?
70 Bottom line
71 Tropical spot
72 Went white
73 In need of middle management?
74 "Bang Bang" singer, 1966

DOWN

1 Groundwork
2 In the air
3 Pre-chrysalis stage
4 Record
5 Call at first
6 Painter Mondrian
7 Is, to Isabella
8 Chili rating unit?
9 Depended
10 Miles from Plymouth
11 Boxing punch
12 Few and far between
13 Hammett pooch
14 Excellent, slangily
22 Prefix with thermal
23 Licit
27 Language from which "safari" comes
28 Part of a science course
29 Museum display
31 Final check
32 Ye follower
33 Gas leak giveaway
34 Satanic
35 Endow with authority
36 "Zounds!"
37 Luau favor
39 Fall faller
41 Chewing gum mouthful
43 Masterful
44 Runner with a turned-up nose
50 Victim of ring rot
52 Have title to
53 Parson's place
54 Big shot
56 Molded jelly
57 Collar attachment
58 Top scout
59 Have the tiller
60 Fab Four film
61 Part of the eye
62 Square thing
63 Learning method
64 "___ corny . . ."
65 Up to snuff

by Richard Silvestri

ACROSS

1 Mountain goat's spot
5 Letter-shaped fastener
10 Shake up
14 Hold sway
15 "Socrate" composer
16 Co. bigwig
17 "You said it!"
18 Dress design
19 "Jaywalking" personality
20 Smash
23 Pipe type
24 Once-common skyline sights
28 Head of state?
29 Athlete seated at a table, maybe
33 "Shrek" princess
34 "It's Impossible" crooner
35 Advice to a Harley passenger
39 Cracked a bit
41 County near Tyrone
42 Fits perfectly
46 Jiffy
49 Soccer forward
50 Put on
52 Sprint to the tape . . . and a hint to this puzzle's theme
56 Pacific retreat
59 Like any of seven Nolan Ryan games
60 Similar
61 Tom Joad, for one
62 With 57-Down, 1950s campaign slogan

63 Hawaii's state bird
64 Does a dog trick
65 Break off
66 Windsor, for one

DOWN

1 Tarzan portrayer
2 They spread fast
3 Joan's "Dynasty" role
4 Salami variety
5 B-1 letters
6 Hope/Crosby "Road" destination
7 Ear-related
8 Going from A to B, say
9 [Giggle]
10 Suffered from an allergy, maybe
11 Send packing
12 Meditative sect
13 "Foucault's Pendulum" author
21 Hardly robust
22 Employer of many auditors: Abbr.
25 Plenty
26 Apollo vehicle, for short
27 Good sign for an angel
30 Retinal cell
31 Phone trigram
32 Fish in a John Cleese film
33 Enriches with vitamins
35 "Aquarius" musical
36 Asian holiday

37 High dudgeon
38 Destined for the record books
39 Onager
40 Stick out
43 Do moguls, say
44 Court action
45 A.L. East player
46 Not tacit
47 Cause of weird weather
48 Young swan
51 Short-sheeting, e.g.
53 Weapon in a rumble
54 Scout outing
55 Poll closing?
56 Watch attachment
57 See 62-Across
58 Energetic dance

by Alan Arbesfeld

ACROSS

1 "That stinks!," quaintly
4 Ladder danger
8 It makes Frisky frisky
14 Evangelical sch. with a 4,000+ enrollment
15 On the deep
16 Top gun
17 Alternative to Gleem
18 "Pretty Woman" and "Waiting to Exhale"
20 Shul's shepherd
22 On its way
23 Stew (over)
24 Shepherds' locales
26 Like harp seals
28 Actor who got his start on TV's "Gimme a Break!"
32 Roadie's load
33 "Master"
34 "I Love Lucy" costar
38 Wing, e.g.
40 Archie Bunker, famously
42 Belgrade resident
43 Dummy Mortimer
45 Hit Sega title character
47 Gene material
48 Shooter of westerns
51 What virgin drinks lack
54 1847 novel subtitled "A Narrative of Adventures in the South Seas"
55 Gladly
56 Oscar-winning role for Helen Mirren, in brief
59 Part of a metropolitan area
62 They're exercised when cycling
65 ___ Canals
66 Rival of Old El Paso
67 Opera's ___ Te Kanawa
68 Useful insect secretion
69 Not just hypothesize
70 It's hard to believe
71 Singer Sumac

DOWN

1 Animal hunted in one of Hercules' 12 labors
2 ___ da capo
3 It's embarrassing to eat
4 Spa offerings
5 Tree of life, in Norse myth
6 Kauai keepsakes
7 Some needlework
8 Beach cover-up
9 Be indisposed
10 Those who don't behave seriously
11 Mother-of-pearl
12 Clinton adviser Harold
13 Termites and such
19 Patella
21 Old Turkish title
25 Fashion designer Elie
27 Pioneer in 33⅓ r.p.m. records
28 Photocopier woes
29 Land on the end of a peninsula
30 Sounds from a teakettle
31 Ordeal's quality
35 With shaking hands, perhaps
36 "Rule, Britannia" composer
37 Letter-shaped beam
39 Automatic-drip machine maker
41 Busy viewer's convenience
44 "What an idiot I am!"
46 Arrives
49 Plumlike Chinese fruit
50 Fish eaten cold
51 Foil-making giant
52 Specialists in storytelling?
53 Druids, e.g.
57 Totally gross
58 Pelvic bones
60 Go far and wide
61 Part of Florida's Gold Coast, informally
63 Restaurant V.I.P.: Abbr.
64 Misreckon

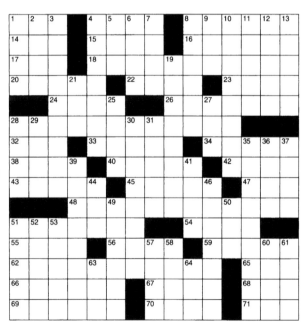

by Stella Daily and Bruce Venzke

Note: The answers to the 13 starred clues have something in common.

ACROSS

1 *Stone in Hollywood
7 *Home for Will Rogers and Garth Brooks
15 1950s All-Star outfielder Minnie
16 *What some unscrupulous e-businesses do?
17 Arthurian paradise
18 Bejeweled pendant
19 *Torn
20 Regatta crew leaders
21 Govt. code-breaking group
22 Wish to take back
23 Song syllable
25 U.S. mil. medal
27 Whence the line "A soft answer turneth away wrath"
31 *Extremely narrow winning margin
35 *Kind of club
37 Mother of Queen Elizabeth I
38 Lingerie shade
41 *A Perón
42 Mercury model
43 TV Dr. of note
44 *Student of Dr. Pangloss
46 *Lover of Radames
47 Like some nursery care
50 Cape Town's country: Abbr.
53 Oz. and kg.
54 Washington ballplayer, briefly
56 Study
59 Class __
62 *Renown
63 Nullify
65 Air __
67 *Site of much horsing around?

68 Architectural decoration
69 *Perform ostentatiously
70 *Destiny

DOWN

1 Astrologer Sydney
2 Meet, as expectations, with "to"
3 Goofier
4 Battery unit
5 That, in Tijuana
6 Friend of Harry and Hermione
7 Capital near the 60th parallel
8 2001 film set in a mental institution
9 Washed
10 Collect

11 Anthropomorphic cinema computer
12 Lena of "Chocolat"
13 Place to which Bart Simpson makes prank calls
14 Gillette brand
20 Dodge on the road
23 New Deal program, for short
24 Renaissance instrument
26 Home in the Alps
28 Eyepiece
29 Curer of feta cheese
30 Lay
32 Even one
33 Wayfarer's stop
34 King's title
36 Sully
38 Clean Air Act org.
39 The Bears, on scoreboards

40 Completely free
45 Some "Law & Order" figs.
48 Ancient garland
49 Kind of class
51 Cancel
52 __ Viejo (California city near Laguna Beach)
55 Creed element
56 Medics
57 Cole Porter's "Well, Did You __?"
58 "Quo Vadis" role
60 Old music halls
61 Result of a whipping
62 End-of-wk. times
64 Big fight
65 1991 film directed by 1-Across
66 "Either he goes __ go!"

by Lee Glickstein and Craig Kasper

ACROSS

1 A diehard enemy might want yours
6 Gather
11 QB's goals
14 Amor vincit ___
15 Milk: Prefix
16 In
17 Call in roulette
19 Suffix with fish
20 For smaller government, presumably
21 One who supplies the means
23 Knocks off
25 Gun dealer's stock
26 Norway's patron saint
30 Call in blackjack
34 Robot maid on "The Jetsons"
36 Buttresses
37 Call in many a betting game
44 Impart
45 Broadcast portion
46 Call in draw poker
52 John P. Marquand detective
53 Signify
54 Prefix with carpal
56 Sounds of walking in moccasins
60 Deicing tool
65 Detroit-to-Philadelphia dir.
66 Call in craps
68 Family room
69 Challenge to ___
70 Family girl
71 Inexact fig.

72 Request to meet in person
73 Photographer Adams

DOWN

1 It has arms, legs and a back
2 "Let's go!"
3 "Sometimes you feel like ___ . . ."
4 Italian river valley in W.W. II fighting
5 Page of music
6 Cosmonaut Leonov, the first human to walk in space
7 "Holy moly!"
8 Fair-sized plot
9 Old British gun
10 Fountain offering
11 1991 Geena Davis title role

12 "The Sound of Music" hit
13 "Sophie's Choice" author
18 Per
22 Catch
24 Celebrity
26 Fort ___ on Monterey Bay
27 W.C.
28 Tempe sch.
29 Tiny tale
31 Part of r.p.m.: Abbr.
32 Pre-1868 Tokyo
33 Dog in 1930s films
35 Fitzgerald who sang "A-Tisket, A-Tasket"
38 Comics cry
39 Start of long-distance dialing

40 Make music on a comb
41 Answer before exchanging rings
42 Have a ___ to pick
43 Sentimental drivel
46 Hinder
47 Some auto deals
48 Present but not active
49 Contents of some shells
50 Be cozy
51 Write permanently
55 Rock concert setting
57 Pitchers' stats
58 Depended (on)
59 Pivot
61 Score after deuce
62 Bakery display
63 "___ homo"
64 Line holder
67 NASA vehicle

by Robert Dillman

ACROSS

1 C-shaped gadget
6 Breastplate, e.g.
11 "Kinda" suffix
14 Spokes, essentially
15 Break from service
16 E-file preparer, briefly
17 Good-looking, briefly
19 Part of a confession
20 Oscar winner Tomei
21 Like a woodland
23 Inventor Rubik
24 Bounty letters
26 Thumbscrew ridges
27 Final Four org.
29 Dom or earl
30 Low man
33 Taylor Hicks, e.g.
35 Sharp as a tack
38 Cable network owned by NBC Universal
39 Oh-so-cute carnival prizes, briefly
42 Pirouette pivot
43 Adoption agcy.
45 Projector unit
46 "Jerusalem Delivered" poet
48 Of yore
50 Fall setting
52 Dry rot, e.g.
54 Bustle
55 "Don't forget . . ."
59 Prayer wheel inscriptions
61 "Oops!" list
63 Phoenix-to-Albuquerque dir.
64 Risky person to do business with, briefly

66 Holy ones: Abbr.
67 Made public
68 Possessive pronoun in an old hymn
69 It may be cocked
70 Some are proper
71 Church assembly

DOWN

1 ___ fraîche
2 Agent Swifty
3 Deck out
4 Flunkies
5 Places to refuel
6 Toby filler
7 Marine hazards
8 Deli supply
9 It's too much
10 Take umbrage at

11 Winter hazards, briefly
12 Hawker's line
13 Deck crew
18 "That's a laugh!"
22 Be a sourpuss
25 Fair one?
28 "Le ___ d'Or"
29 Rang out
30 H.O.V. lane user
31 Shakespeare's "poor venomous fool"
32 Student writing competition, briefly
34 Buck's mate
36 Aurora, to the Greeks
37 Opposite of paleo-

40 Fortress of old
41 Sault ___ Marie Canals
44 Kelp, for one
47 Possible result of a natural disaster
49 Victim of Macbeth
51 Active sort
52 Crayola color changed to "peach"
53 ___ Mountains, home of King's Peak
54 Ghostly pale
56 Like most South Americans
57 Note taker
58 Propelled a shell
60 Hose shade
62 Mafiosi who "flip"
65 Online revenue sources

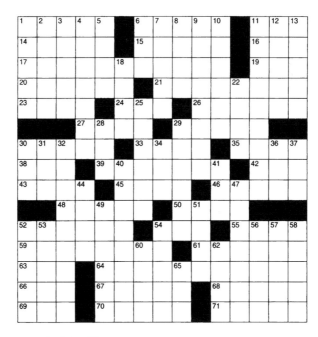

by Robert Zimmerman

ACROSS

1 The Velvet Fog
6 Casino pair
10 Cabaret, e.g.
14 Smuggler's stock
15 Giant-screen film format
16 Summer wine selection
17 All the rockets in existence?
20 Ask for
21 Some emergency cases, for short
22 Place for shots
23 Noughts-and-crosses win
25 Brand of shaving products
26 "Dry-clean only," e.g.?
33 Empty (of)
34 Small, as a Beanie Baby
35 First course option
36 Does as told
38 ___ Andreas fault
39 Like déjà vu
40 Turner who sang "The Best"
41 Marzipan ingredient
43 Piggy
44 Cooking utensil from central Spain?
47 Like a starless sky
48 Alt. spelling
49 Iran-___
52 Debtor's letters
54 ___ buco
58 HAL 9000, in "2001: A Space Odyssey"?
61 First-year J.D. candidate
62 Restaurant chain acronym
63 Thus far
64 A sergeant might ask a soldier to pick it up

65 I.R.S. ID's
66 Recipe parts

DOWN

1 Tabbies' mates
2 Mayberry boy
3 Angry reaction
4 Animal with a shaggy coat
5 U.K. record label
6 Fizzled out
7 Radio's "___ in the Morning"
8 Poky
9 Mutual fund redemption charge
10 Deep fissure
11 Oral history
12 "Evil empire" of the '80s
13 "It's ___ real!"
18 Sarge's superior

19 Brewery units
24 Baseball's Ed and Mel
25 Relative key of C major
26 Second-longest human bone
27 Utopias
28 Stahl of "60 Minutes"
29 As a friend, to the French
30 Outlet of the left ventricle
31 Astronaut ___ Bluford, the first African-American in space
32 Sport with lunges
33 Mil. option
37 First N.F.L. QB with consecutive 30-touchdown passing seasons

39 Novelist Ferber
41 Acid neutralizers
42 "___ Organum" (1620 Francis Bacon work)
45 Crucifix inscription
46 Subject of the 1999 film "Le Temps Retrouvé"
49 Karate blow
50 The last Mrs. Chaplin
51 Minute part of a minute: Abbr.
52 A program usually has one
53 "Stupid me!"
55 Eyelid woe
56 Ooze
57 Table scraps
59 Geezers' replies
60 Dads

by Paula Gamache

ACROSS

1 7-Up flavor
5 Easter serving
9 Funny ones
14 "Just ___!"
15 Succulent plant
16 Clinker
17 Locker room supply
18 *Solid ground
20 *You should have the body
22 Online currency
23 Catches in the act
24 Pro at balancing
27 Big pet food brand
30 Pageant wear
32 Erica who wrote "Any Woman's Blues"
35 Bottom of a lily
38 Bank rights
39 Schoenberg's "Moses und ___"
40 *From the beginning
42 Gray-brown goose
43 "The Taming of the Shrew" setting
45 Sport whose name means "gentle way"
46 Formerly, once
47 Kind of number
49 7'1" N.B.A. star, informally
51 Pince-___
52 Shout to a team, maybe
55 Fall colors
59 *The die is cast
62 *Always the same
65 "Warm"
66 They're rather pointless
67 "Camelot" actor Franco

68 Other, in the barrio
69 Charges
70 Innovative 1982 Disney film
71 Like a busybody

DOWN

1 Wood-turning tool
2 Stern that bows
3 Nellie of opera
4 *Behold the proof
5 Back muscles, for short
6 "The Black Stallion" boy
7 Idiot
8 He said "Slump? I ain't in no slump. I just ain't hitting"
9 Turndown

10 Van Gogh floral subject
11 Bobby of Boston
12 Male cat
13 Title in S. Amer.
19 Getaway alerts, for short
21 Cry before "It's you!"
24 All alternative
25 ___ Grove, N.J.
26 Money in the bank, e.g.
28 Part of a C.E.O.'s résumé
29 Topic: Abbr.
31 *Without which not
32 Black lacquer
33 Filibuster, in a way
34 Alertness aid

36 Bud's comedy sidekick
37 Briefs, briefly
41 "Isn't that beautiful?!"
44 Lacking purpose
48 Round dance official
50 Gallery display
53 Canonized figure
54 One who's not "it"
56 Look after
57 Some Peters
58 Homeless animal
59 Mimicked
60 Pertaining to flying
61 "Follow me!"
62 Leave in stitches?
63 Air quality org.
64 Debussy's "La ___"

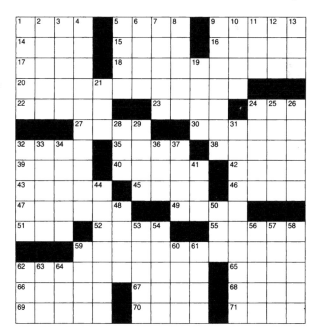

by Patrick Blindauer

ACROSS

1 Big stingers
6 Johnny Fever's workplace, in 1970s–'80s TV
10 Amt. at a car dealership
14 Ancient marketplace
15 Mixed bag
16 Siouan tribe
17 Some horizontal lines
18 Carries
19 Birthstone of someone born on Halloween
20 Professional secrets
23 Muslim holy man
26 Amanda of "The Whole Nine Yards"
27 Off-site meetings, maybe
28 Promoted, as a pawn
30 Took to court
32 Went bad
33 Formal discourse
34 "Choosy moms choose __"
37 Ham it up
38 __ pop
39 Ride the __ (sit out a baseball game)
40 Heros
41 Red in the middle
42 Large, at Starbucks
43 Elec. Day, e.g.
44 Hockey feat
45 Some urban legends
46 Aussie's neighbor
47 Like some old stores
48 Early seventh-century year
50 Wander
52 Whirlpool
53 U.N. ambassador under Reagan
56 Shows
57 Entr'__
58 Certain flower girl
62 Focal point
63 Honolulu's home
64 Reese of "Touched by an Angel"
65 Plea
66 Swill
67 Balance sheet listing

DOWN

1 Candle material
2 Turkish title
3 Red __
4 Stain looseners on washday
5 Lip
6 Gobbled up, with "down"
7 Movie for which Jane Fonda won an Oscar
8 Starboard
9 You might strike one
10 Docked
11 Mid-March honoree
12 Map lines
13 New York Cosmos star
21 Like some columns
22 Fig or fir
23 Hurdle for Mensa membership
24 Hawaiian dress
25 Organism needing oxygen
29 Born
31 Can. neighbor
33 Something said while holding a bag
34 Having bad luck, say
35 Mean
36 Spunky
38 Like The Onion
39 War enders
41 Uncooked
42 Designer Diane __ Furstenberg
44 Honey site
45 Rope material
46 "Sexual Behavior in the Human Male" author
47 Begin, as a hobby
48 Two-sport Sanders
49 Entertainment from a magician
51 Brand name in lawn care
53 Chimpanzee researcher Goodall
54 "Get Smart" org.
55 ". . . __ bottle of rum"
59 Choices for Chicago commuters
60 Cavs, on a scoreboard
61 Nag (at)

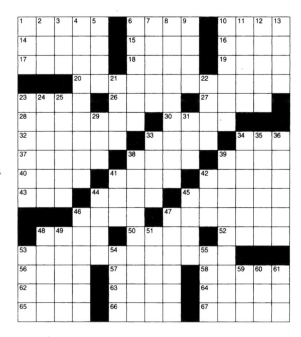

by Ken Stern

ACROSS

1 Scores, as a victory, with "up"
7 Blunted blade
11 Hipster
14 Door sign
15 Fancy club trophies
16 Pale ___
17 Mongol horde, e.g.
18 Romantic goings-on
20 "Rose is a rose is a rose is a rose" writer
21 Clinton cabinet member
22 Poetic land
23 Tupperware sale event
25 Takes a turn
26 City limits sign abbr.
27 Dept. of Labor agcy.
29 N.L. Central team
32 Society column word
34 Erie Canal city
38 What 18-, 23-, 55- and 63-Across each comprises
43 Early time to rise
44 Mahmoud Abbas's grp.
45 Pro-gun org.
46 Catches Z's
49 Star pitchers
52 Chorus after a bad call
55 Catching cold?
60 Annika Sorenstam's org.
61 Fraternity letters
62 Good-looker
63 Cockpit datum
65 Whodunit plot element

66 Vane dir.
67 "You lookin' ___?"
68 Spring bloomers
69 ___ Moines
70 North Sea feeder
71 When many stores open

DOWN

1 Don't go together
2 Must
3 It means "Go with God"
4 Act as a go-between
5 Boarding site
6 Sound of a leak
7 Calculus pioneer
8 Chop-chop
9 Embassy figures

10 Suffix with Brooklyn
11 Where "Aida" premiered
12 Jude Law title role
13 Many Justin Timberlake fans
19 Smooth, musically
21 Was incoherent
24 "All the King's Men" star, 2006
28 Important airport
29 They cross aves.
30 ___-night doubleheader
31 Deli delicacy
33 Eerie ability
35 Novelist Fleming
36 N.B.A. position: Abbr.

37 "___ friend, I . . ."
39 Toto's home
40 "___ Believer"
41 Five Norse kings
42 Points that may have rays
47 Lab tubes
48 Intrigue
50 Debutante's date
51 Confined
52 Short on flavor
53 Say one's piece
54 Shrek's ilk
56 Pillow filler
57 Answer to "Who's there?"
58 David of Pink Panther movies
59 Foie gras sources
64 Pony up
65 "Mamma ___!"

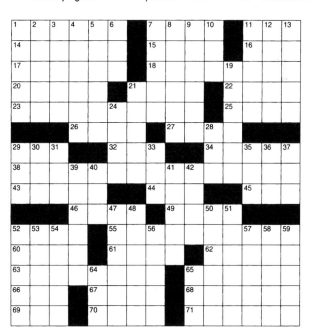

by Richard Chisholm

The clues in this puzzle appear in a single list, combining Across and Down. Where two answers share a number, the unclued Down answer is a homophone of the corresponding Across answer.

CLUES

1 Obstruction at the entrance to a cave, maybe
2 Rarely used golf club
3 Picture on a $50 bill
4 Drip, say
5 Seventh-century year
6 Want ad abbr.
7 Some needle holders, for short
8 Like jail cells
9 Makes like
10 Connecticut or Colorado: Abbr.
11 Touch up, as a painting
12 Country named for its location on the globe
13 Bring down
14 Having hit a double
15 Neuter
16 For one
17 Party of the first part and party of the second part, e.g.
18 Gets going
19 Weapon in old hand-to-hand fighting
20 Does some yard work
21 One famously begins "O Wild West Wind, thou breath of Autumn's being"
22 Carcinogenic substance
23 Victorian ___
24 Headquartered
25 Lowers the cuffs on, maybe

26 Legis. period
27 Point to
28 Wood of the Rolling Stones
29 ___ Nikolaevich, last czarevitch of Russia
30 Queen of France in Shakespeare's "Henry V"
31 Rich Spanish decorations
32 Big blasts, informally
33 Duck down
34 Tailors
35 Social register listees
36 Residents: Suffix
37 Seat at a hootenanny
38 Place for a guard

39 Recondite
40 Shoulder muscle
41 Tolerates
42 Logged
43 Singer who founded Reprise Records
44 Letter before Peter in old radio lingo
45 Bygone council
46 Donations at some clinics
47 Essential
48 "___ for nest"
49 Accent
50 NASA subj.
51 French town
52 Contents of some shells

53 Audio equipment pioneer
54 Wiped out
55 Verb of which "sum" is a form
56 Campsite visitor
57 Job specifications
58 ___ B. Wells, early civil rights advocate
59 Individually
60 Race unit
61 Blood type letters
62 Calculator button
63 Wears down
64 Work force
65 Grade again
66 Pretended to be

by Joe Krozel

ACROSS

1 Seinfeld's "sworn enemy"
7 En route
15 Dig up
16 Vicious sorts
17 1961 Connie Francis hit
19 Up to no good
20 Sterile, in a way
21 Debussy's "Air de ___"
22 Word before Oscar or Orloff
24 Madras title
25 Intl. agreement since 1993
27 Class-conscious grps.?
29 Prefix with skeleton
32 Hold 'em challenge
34 Fourth book of the Book of Mormon
36 Gore follower
37 Eponymous rink jump
39 Bring up
41 View from Long Is.
42 Tennyson woman called "the Fair"
44 ___ Beach, Fla.
45 ___ Jordan, who wrote "The Crying Game"
47 A writer may work on it
49 Bolero, e.g.
50 Long on screen
52 First name in architecture
54 One-third of a Morse "O"
55 Children's author/photographer Alda
58 "Here, I can help you"
61 End of a line about "friends"

63 Not be honest about oneself
64 Ingredients in many stews
65 Derides
66 Become, as mush

DOWN

1 Google heading
2 Thrill
3 1952 Doris Day hit that was an even bigger hit for the Lettermen in 1961
4 ___ acid (old name for hydrochloric acid)
5 Bob ___, young man in Dreiser's "Sister Carrie"
6 Web-based service
7 Be in charge of

8 Pointed extremity
9 Suffix with beta
10 First sitting president to visit the West Coast
11 Protect
12 "Huh?!"
13 It rises in the Bernese Alps
14 Battle of the ___, 1914
18 Mr. Wickfield's clerk, in literature
23 Narrow way
25 Passover month
26 Gentleman of the court
28 "Deal!"
30 Troop group
31 Kind of daisy

33 Eternities
35 Starting point
38 Efface, with "off"
40 One of the men waiting in "Waiting for Godot"
43 Like some eyes
46 Mortgagor, e.g.
48 Canadian native
51 At hand, in poems
53 Optional phrase
55 Belt-hole makers
56 Nose: Prefix
57 Reef dwellers
59 Button on an iPod
60 Sinclair alternative
62 Part of una semana

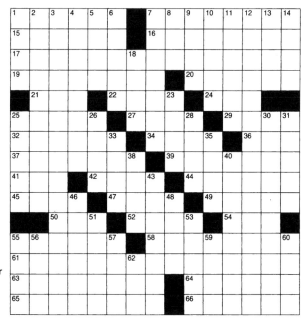

by Victor Fleming and Bruce Venzke

ACROSS

1 Burns's tongue
6 Popular desktops since 1998
11 Camel's end?
14 Cul-de-sac
15 Wearer of the Yankees' retired #9
16 3.2 million-member org. with a pi in its logo
17 Wardrobe malfunction?
19 Atlantic City hotel, informally, with "the"
20 "Blah blah blah blah blah"
21 Start of a musical scale
22 Arias, usually
23 "___ Time" (1952 million-selling Eddie Fisher hit)
24 Unit of punishment
26 Result of punishment
28 Mood after a military victory?
32 Polling results, e.g.
35 Tries
36 Beastly
39 Ranges
40 Akin
42 Estuaries
43 Where porcine pilots arrive?
46 Narc's discovery, maybe
47 Believed
48 Grand Canyon area
51 Early English actress Nell ___
53 Not just threaten
55 Threats to World War shipping
57 Certain southeast Asian
58 Hint to 17-, 28- and 43-Across

60 Hospital dept.
61 YouTube feature
62 Hardly futuristic
63 A.L. city, on scoreboards
64 A lot
65 Beaker

DOWN

1 Kind of tank
2 First name in late-night
3 Over near
4 Old New York paper, for short
5 Artist Frank ___, pioneer in Minimalism
6 Org. that lends to countries
7 Arrive with authority

8 Nickname among major-league sluggers
9 It has many pictures
10 Boomer, once
11 Director Michelangelo
12 Warranty feature
13 Muslim honorific
18 "___ me"
22 Emmy-winning Phil
25 Trial position, for short
27 Like ___ out of hell
28 Late editorial cartoonist Bill
29 Carol starter
30 Abbr. on an envelope to Mexico
31 Flat sound
32 Radio feature
33 Eleanor Roosevelt's first name

34 Certain notes
37 Work hard
38 Doubter
41 Like wedding attendees, often
44 "___ U"
45 Tennis great Stefan
48 Dreadlocks wearer
49 Anatomical passages
50 Old PC standard
51 Smooth
52 "Cross the Brazos at ___" (1964 country hit)
54 ___-approved
56 Turgenev's home in Russia
58 Emergency rm. sights
59 Sister of Helios

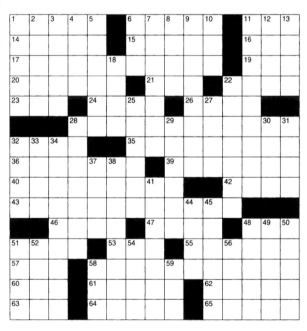

by Daniel C. Bryant

ACROSS

1 Times to call, in some classifieds
4 Johnny Carson persona
9 Sauce
14 Serious crimes
17 Perry Mason line
18 Crest bearer in heraldry
19 Showed enthusiasm for, with "up"
20 Highest bond rating
21 Passes more than once
24 Annually
26 "___ Robin Gray" (classic Scottish ballad)
28 Dr. ___ Schneider, historian who was a love interest of Indiana Jones
32 Order sought by an accused before trial
39 Hearing, e.g.
40 Lawyers' requests at trials
41 You are, in Aragón
42 De bene ___ (of conditional validity)
43 Kind of hand
47 Title locale in a Cheech Marin film
52 Neighbor of Libya: Abbr.
55 Energy
56 Hombres en la familia
57 Equals at a trial
63 Specialist's offering
64 Snappish
65 Relative of -ish
66 ___ Tamid (synagogue lamp)

DOWN

1 Part of a company
2 Family name in Olympic skiing
3 Period of time
4 Montréal's Rue ___-Catherine
5 Erstwhile military aux.
6 Drink in "The Taming of the Shrew"
7 "Hey, ___!" (Jamaican greeting)
8 Suppose
9 First multiracial coeducational college in the South
10 Night stand leader?
11 Mythical mount
12 Certain sorority woman
13 What she is in Italy
15 Bean sprout?
16 Grand affair
22 Meal, in Milan
23 Lazy ___
24 Like many pets
25 Steel support for concrete
27 Kissers
29 Legal scholar Guinier
30 Twisted
31 On the less windy side
32 Crown
33 Entrance
34 Remote option
35 Lucky sorts?
36 Modernists
37 French cup
38 "Coffee ___?"
44 Key component
45 Falling-out
46 Overplay
48 The brain has one
49 Fastenable, as labels
50 Emmy-winning Michaels
51 From Nineveh: Abbr.
52 "Leaving on ___ Plane"
53 Elegance
54 Assns. and orgs.
58 Still
59 Old video game inits.
60 Abbr. on a firm's letterhead
61 Good name for a flight attendant?
62 Bake sale offering

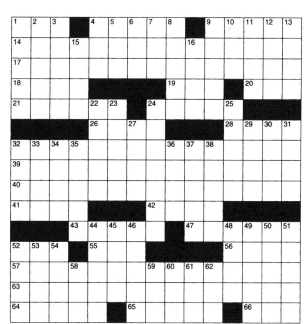

by Joe Krozel and Victor Fleming

ACROSS

1 "Wait ___!"
5 Terrif
10 Andrew of "Melrose Place"
14 Longtime Vicki Lawrence character
15 Burn slowly
16 One of the Munsters
17 Popular depilatory
18 Static
19 Baryshnikov's birthplace
20 "Jolly good!"
22 Pioneer in I.Q. testing
23 Honoraria
24 Takeout choice
26 Home of São Miguel Island
29 Lab container
30 British general in the American Revolution
31 Light-colored stogie
32 Dallas-to-Austin dir.
35 Author of a 1952 novel published in full in Life magazine
39 "No ___!"
40 Occupy
41 Nutritionist Paul who founded a pet food company
42 Pear-shaped instrument
43 Rodeo sights
45 "I"-opening experience?
48 Throw out water
49 Ticks off
50 Accessory for many a game
54 Winnebago owner
55 Amber, e.g.
57 Height
58 Like llamas
59 Truck stop sign
60 Unpleasant feeling
61 Some personal data: Abbr.
62 A Stooge
63 Many a D.C. org.

DOWN

1 Peloponnesian War participant
2 Part of a Three Stooges shtick
3 Dr. Skoda of "Law & Order"
4 Happy-go-lucky
5 Elvis's "Hound Dog" and "Anyway You Want Me"
6 Some chain hotels
7 Gave up one's hand
8 Suffix with two
9 Morsel
10 3-Down's profession
11 German poet who wrote "Don't send a poet to London"
12 Presses
13 Flow out
21 Formerly known as
22 Animal on the backs of three state quarters
24 Surgical aid
25 Mata ___
26 Faux cough
27 Author ___ Neale Hurston
28 Fesses (up to)
29 Part of un jardin
31 Badly made
32 End of a fly? . . . or the start of one?
33 All the ___
34 "The Swiss Family Robinson" author Johann
36 Rouses oneself
37 South American monkey
38 Politician who wrote the book "Leadership"
42 Rears
43 Oscar winner for "Yankee Doodle Dandy"
44 Baseball datum
45 Odd jobs
46 Buckles
47 Ingredient in some potato chips
48 Old nightclub employee
50 Old Testament book
51 Thom ___ shoes
52 Layers of eggs weighing more than a pound
53 Move to first class, e.g.
55 Boombox button
56 Evian or Perrier

by Alex Boisvert

ACROSS

1 End of many college addresses
7 Fictional pirate
11 Suffix with official
14 "I do," e.g.
15 King's position, in a game
16 "Another Green World" musician
17 90
19 The Silver State: Abbr.
20 Like white elephants
21 Damp basement cause
23 One way to stand
26 Prime Cuts maker
28 This and that
29 Shia leaders
32 3
35 Jai alai ball
37 Lake ___
38 1
43 Present-day Persian
44 Don't stop
45 7
49 Criticize sneakily
50 Skittles variety
51 Weary worker's cry
53 Roll call call
54 Auto accident sound
57 Cruise ship Empress of the ___
60 Turner in the Rock and Roll Hall of Fame
61 What is being held in 17-, 32-, 38- and 45-Across
66 Receive
67 Captain of literature
68 "The Power and the Glory" novelist, 1940
69 Walletful, informally

70 Like many games
71 Hunter-gatherer types

DOWN

1 Drop bait lightly on the water
2 Eggs in labs
3 A.L. team, on scoreboards
4 Still-life object
5 Carvey of "Wayne's World"
6 Extreme sort
7 Alan Jay Lerner's "___ Wasn't You"
8 ___ Valley Conference in college sports
9 Gen. Robt. ___
10 Alternatively
11 20,320-foot Alaskan peak
12 Capacity of many a flash drive, informally
13 Not dawdle
18 Information desk offering
22 Some carriers
23 Old King Cole accessory
24 Kind of card
25 Soapstone, e.g.
27 Plant nursery activity
30 Pseudonym of Jean Baptiste Poquelin
31 ___ Report of the 1990s
33 Breakfast place
34 Beach sights
36 Second in a Latin series
39 Damned one

40 Samoan capital
41 Like some muscles
42 Common injury site
45 Franciscan locale
46 Unpopular, in a way
47 Makes applesauce, e.g.
48 One helping
52 Pretend
55 Locale of many Italian vineyards
56 Bawl (out)
58 It's rarely seen under a hat
59 Originate
62 Sauce ingredient
63 Mauna ___
64 Culmination
65 "You bet!"

by Peter Wentz

ACROSS

1 Twinge
5 W.W. II blast makers
11 Realm of Proteus, in Greek myth
14 ___ patriae
15 Pack again, as hay
16 ___ Rose
17 Leading Russian in the 32-Down
19 One to one, e.g.
20 Regard
21 Attitudes
23 Pilgrim in Chaucer's "The Canterbury Tales"
24 Florida island resort
25 Once, once
27 Prayer word
30 Paul McCartney played it for the Beatles
33 NASA launch vehicle
36 Record producer Davis
37 Connection for an electric guitar
38 Newsmaker of October 4, 1957
40 Result of a road emergency
41 Be hot under the collar
43 New Mexico county or its seat
44 Basted
45 Orders
46 Korea's Syngman
48 "20 Hrs., 40 Min." author, 1928
52 Catch on the range
56 Detroit suburb named for the plants the area was once overgrown with
58 Blocked, as a harbor, with "up"
59 Victorian ___
60 Leading American in the 32-Down

62 Twitch
63 Personally handle
64 Egg on
65 Bridge topper?
66 Finishes
67 Earl, for one

DOWN

1 One with checks and balances?
2 Beguile
3 Durango direction
4 Distresses
5 Composer Khachaturian
6 Have a hand out, say
7 Future senator who delivered the 2004 Democratic convention keynote address
8 California county
9 Shrovetide dish
10 Remit
11 38-Across, e.g.
12 "No ___"
13 Stein fillers
18 "The Waltons" actor
22 Dump, e.g.
24 Show pride, in a way
26 Bonehead
28 Profess
29 Chopped
30 Odist, e.g.
31 Parisian possessive
32 Event started by 38-Across
34 ___ Pi (dessert lover's fraternity?)
35 Stallion's sound
38 Enterprise log entry
39 Suffix with sheep or goat

42 1972 Wimbledon winner Smith
44 Arctic newborn
47 First name at the 1986 Nobel Prize ceremony
49 Van ___
50 "___ flowing with milk and honey" (Canaan, in the Bible)
51 Tears
53 Intimidate, in a way, with "down"
54 Suit material
55 Comparatively unconventional
56 Kind of cheese
57 Newsman Sevareid
58 Butcher's, baker's or candlestick maker's
61 Disco guy on "The Simpsons"

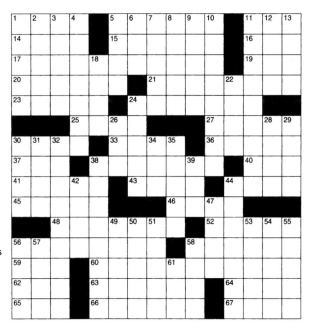

by Sheldon Benardo

ACROSS

1 Any one of a trio of Hollywood sisters
6 Reason to get some cosmetic dental work
10 ___-Americans (about 3.5 million people)
14 Say "amen," say
15 Gadzooks, e.g.
16 "You've Got Mail" actress
17 People's 2006 Sexiest Man Alive
19 Just
20 City southeast of 64-Across
21 Starting
22 Beverage brand
24 Mouth's locale
26 Cage for hawks
27 Subway stop: Abbr.
28 New York's ___ Mansion
30 Hen, e.g.
32 Julius Caesar portrayer, 1963
34 What a drinker may enter
38 Chevrolet model
39 Big exporter of coconut cream and coconut oil
41 Prefix with kinetic
42 O.K.'s
44 Frat Pack actor
46 Tasty
48 Smirk
49 Fertilized things
52 Wander
53 Like some checks
54 Quarter
56 City with una torre pendente
57 Particularly: Abbr.
60 R & B singer with a hit 1990s sitcom
61 Wishful things? . . . or a literal description of 16-, 17-, 32-, 44- and 60-Across

64 City along the Chisholm Trail
65 Fidel Castro's brother
66 Part of a printing press
67 Refuse
68 Starchy side dish
69 Points on a crescent moon

DOWN

1 Crazy
2 Like relics
3 Timber hewers
4 Poetic contraction
5 Robes, tiaras, etc.
6 Shade of brown
7 Game division
8 "Were ___ do it over . . ."
9 Insincere

10 Partner in an old radio comedy duo
11 Lets
12 Shoelace tip
13 Presidential candidate who said "No one can earn a million dollars honestly"
18 Some organic compounds
23 Water holder
25 Repeats
26 Construction worker
28 South side?
29 French dream
30 Like many cared-for lawns
31 Measure again, as a movie's length
33 Fervent
35 Computer technicians' positions

36 Everyone, in Essen
37 Blast constituent?
40 Historic Umbrian town
43 Palm type
45 Enormous
47 Sauté
49 Like an eyeball
50 "From the Earth to the Moon" author
51 "Encore!"
53 Volleyball stat
55 Annual May event, informally
56 Windfall
58 When repeated, a dance instructor's call
59 Most are 3, 4 or 5
62 Top bond rating
63 Bearded beast

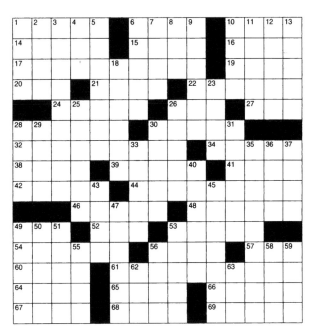

by E. J. Platt

ACROSS

1 Lady abroad
5 With 50-Down, steak go-with
10 With 68-Across, fish filet go-with
14 Wedding parties?: Abbr.
15 Water, for one
16 Tel ___
17 Psyche components
18 Fix, as a hitch
19 Unnerve
20 "Yep" negator
21 Behind closed doors
23 Drug-free
25 Well-founded
29 He-man
33 With 44-Across, hot sandwich go-with
34 Like waves on a shoreline
37 It's on the St. Lawrence River: Abbr.
38 Hilarious . . . or a hint to this puzzle's theme
42 Brown, in ads
43 Passed
44 See 33-Across
47 Closed tight
51 White-knuckle
54 Make a ship stop by facing the wind
55 Newscast lead
59 Drift ___
60 Airline rarity, nowadays
63 "May ___ your order?"
64 Bob Dylan's first wife and the title of a song about her
65 Makeover
66 Stinky
67 Dirty magazines and such

68 See 10-Across
69 See 1-Down
70 Neither good nor bad

DOWN

1 With 69-Across, burger go-with
2 Treat splendidly
3 One saying "I do"
4 Letters before Liberty or Constitution
5 Sprung (from)
6 x, y and z
7 Toy sometimes seen on a beach
8 Order
9 Big name in balers
10 Unisex dress
11 Female gametes
12 1995 showbiz biography by C. David Heymann
13 December 31, e.g.
21 Harden
22 Musician Brian
24 Breezed through
26 One of a series of joint Soviet/U.S. space satellites
27 Dragged out
28 Suffix with absorb
30 Shake, in a way
31 Cable inits. since 1979
32 Albino in "The Da Vinci Code"
35 Police target
36 Jazzy James
38 Something to take in a car
39 Fred Astaire's "___ This a Lovely Day"
40 The Beeb is seen on it
41 "The very ___!"

42 The Rams of the Atlantic 10 Conf.
45 2003 #2 hit for Lil Jon and the East Side Boyz
46 ___-Cat
48 Go-getter
49 Womb
50 See 5-Across
52 Spruce (up)
53 Perfume ingredient
56 1955 Oscar nominee for "Mr. Hulot's Holiday"
57 Tex's neighbor to the north
58 Some wines
60 Partner, informally, with "the"
61 Underwater cave dweller
62 Oral health org.
64 Draft org.

by Lucy Gardner Anderson

ACROSS

1 "Thou art not lovelier than ___, — no" (Millay sonnet start)
7 Make even
10 Neighbor of Afghanistan: Abbr.
13 Cadillac model
14 ___ jam
15 Word with pick or pack
16 With 55-Across, description of 23-, 36- and 44-Across
17 Wither
19 Atlanta's ___ Center
20 College square
22 Playwright Edward and others
23 Beginning of some folk wisdom
26 Clod buster
27 Pacific islands in W.W. II fighting, with "the"
30 Hugh ___, successor to Louis V as king of France
33 Kind of cup
34 Les poissons swim in it
35 Charter
36 Folk wisdom, part 2
37 Doggone
38 Nabokov novel
39 Biblical prophet thrown overboard by his shipmates
40 Formal dress shoes
41 Sane
43 Norwegian coin
44 End of the folk wisdom
49 Obliquely
51 Bishoprics
52 Old Eur. domain
53 Cutout to fill in
55 See 16-Across
57 Additionally
58 Green: Prefix
59 Corrida combatants
60 Have
61 Shade of blue
62 Makeshift hatrack

DOWN

1 ". . . ___ man put asunder" (wedding words)
2 "___ to be alone" (words attributed to Greta Garbo)
3 Wee, quickly
4 Exact proper divisor, in math
5 Part of a contract
6 French legislature
7 Spanish aunt
8 Incised printing method
9 Pendant place
10 Bit of wishful thinking
11 Yearn
12 Phi Beta Kappa mementos
13 Webster's, e.g.: Abbr.
18 Melancholy woodwind
21 Medicinal cardiac stimulant
24 Syngman ___, first president of South Korea
25 The last Pope Paul, e.g.
28 Infield cover
29 Heavenly orbs
30 Scorch
31 She dies with Radames
32 Talk, talk, talk
33 Robert of "The 39 Steps"
36 Teflon, e.g.
37 Any Sonny and Cher song
39 Bumps on a ride
40 Do some advance organizing
42 Ayatollah's home
43 Titania's husband
45 Dividing membranes
46 When doubled, comforting words
47 Cause for an erasure
48 Fighters for Jeff Davis
49 Regarding
50 Pack
54 Powell's co-star in "The Thin Man"
56 Speed: Abbr.

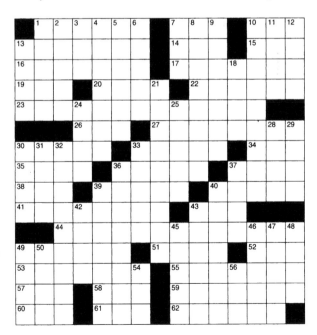

by Susan Harrington Smith

The clues in this puzzle appear in a single list, combining Across and Down. Where two answers share a number, they also share a clue.

CLUES

1 Maintain
2 In ___ (form of research)
3 Concert halls
4 They're unlikely to work
5 Fiddle with
6 Goofed (around)
7 Quod ___ faciendum
8 Negative connector
9 Spy supply
10 Rubberneck
11 Composition of the Spanish Main
12 Hit the road
13 Florida ___
14 Part of Caesar's boast
15 ___ Soleil (Louis XIV)
16 "The Night of the Hunter" screenwriter
17 First name in daredeviltry
18 Some Romanovs
19 Runtish
20 Motor Trend job
21 Prohibition agents
22 Legends
23 Author Jaffe
24 2002 Literature Nobelist ___ Kertész
25 Pair
26 Dodge
27 Sun protection
28 All bark ___ bite
29 Start of a phrase meaning "always"
30 "Sounds like ___!"
31 Gusto
32 Put to rest

33 Changers of 34
34 See 33
35 Cartoon character with feminine wiles
36 Annual parade site
37 Death jokes and such
38 Stamp letters
39 ___ mer
40 Lover of Tess in "Tess of the D'Urbervilles"
41 Part of the Constitution after the Preamble: Abbr.
42 N.F.L. coach who was undefeated in 1972
43 Relative of a cod

44 Like tennis balls and dinners
45 Wicked witch's home in "The Wizard of Oz"
46 Ranch closing?
47 Bowl
48 Comic, e.g.
49 N.F.L. placekicker David
50 Fast-food franchise that started in S. Salt Lake, Ut.
51 Squoosh
52 Impersonator's work
53 It's all downhill from here
54 Gene group
55 "I goofed"
56 Delight
57 Tore
58 Don Juan

59 Old Testament book
60 Cry made with a handshake
61 Nippy
62 Benny Goodman's "___ Foolish Things"
63 Savage
64 Challenge for Theseus, in myth
65 Be a gloomy Gus
66 Radio part
67 Pod holder
68 Something ___ (a wow)
69 Door
70 Unexaggerated

by Larry Shearer

ACROSS
1 Quarrel (with)
5 Contents of a scoop
9 Glass substitute
13 Child's plea
14 "Jabberwocky," for one
15 Real ___
16 Former southern constellation in the shape of a ship
17 Billet-doux writer
18 "Skunk egg"
19 Internal-combustion device
22 Executor's concern
23 When someone 27-Across
27 See 23-Across
30 "Très sexy!"
31 "American Psycho" author
35 One of the first to raise a hand, usually
36 Barn adjunct
37 Scented gift
38 Loser in a staring contest
45 Temper, as metal
46 Vaccine target
47 Acts as a middleman
49 Began
53 Unfeeling nature . . . or a literal hint to 19-, 31- and 38- Across
56 Lustrous black
59 "What ___?"
60 Type choice: Abbr.
61 Apply
62 Not worth ___
63 Equipment in chuck-a-luck
64 Best of the early Beatles
65 Chop ___
66 Tolkien's talking trees

DOWN
1 Suffix with land or sea
2 Setting for "La Traviata"
3 Inner tension
4 It's read to the unruly
5 Beach adjacent to Copacabana
6 The ___ Nugget, Alaska's oldest newspaper
7 Sinn ___
8 The end
9 Historian William H. ___, author of "The Rise of the West"
10 Here, abroad
11 Be lovey-dovey
12 Philosopher Rand
15 Secretary of state during the War of 1812
20 Siouan speaker
21 Monopoly token
24 "Rag Doll" singer, 1964
25 Visitor from afar
26 Kind of surgery for the eyes
28 Home of "Monday Night Football"
29 Soak
31 Without question
32 Marie Antoinette, par exemple
33 Gets
34 Hang ___
39 "You pay attention!"
40 Factor in pageant judging
41 Stewpot
42 One who's late to adopt the latest
43 Leaning
44 Beach maximizer
48 Mex. misses
50 Away
51 Pass
52 Strikes out
54 Vegan's protein source
55 Cartoon canine
56 Agent, for short
57 Sturdy feller?
58 A.S.P.C.A. worker

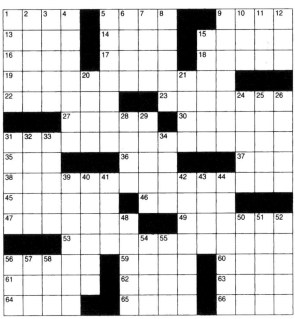

by Paula Gamache

ACROSS

1 "It's all here" sloganeer, once
4 Frisky one
8 Marie Osmond or Loretta Young
14 "Elijah" or "The Creation"
16 Key on a cash register
17 Drop a few positions, maybe
18 Overprotect
19 Maker of Kiwi Teawi
20 Mystery author Dexter
21 The Pacific Ocean's only island kingdom
22 It was good for Sartre
23 One and only
26 They're staffed with doctors
30 Bad time for a tropical vacation
33 Lawyers with many assts.
34 I.T. firm founded by Ross Perot
35 Wine used to make zabaglione
36 Soviet ___
37 Member of an extended familia
38 Country that won the most medals at the 1980 Winter Olympics
40 Reluctantly accepting
42 First name in cosmonautics
43 Major U.S. Spanish-language daily
44 Rarely written-out Latin phrase
48 "Wozzeck" composer ___ Berg
50 What stare decisis upholds the validity of
52 Red line?
54 Set of guidelines

55 Mrs. Tony Blair
56 Put forward
57 Has trouble sleeping, maybe
58 ___ Ramsay ("The Black Stallion" hero)
59 Sorry

DOWN

1 Continue effortlessly
2 Dog in Disney's "Cinderella"
3 "Paradise Lost" character
4 Ultraloyal employees
5 Passed on by taletellers
6 Not full-bodied
7 Wingtip tip
8 Feeling no better
9 "Man is a ___-using animal": Thomas Carlyle

10 Pass under the basket, maybe
11 Is clueless
12 Stout alternative
13 Drift boat attachment
15 Highest-grossing film of 1986
20 Bridesmaid's accessory
22 Very disagreeable
24 Hear
25 Analytic work
27 Soul singer who is also a coronated king of Ghana
28 New rendering
29 Near the bottom of the drawers?
30 Take one more shot at
31 It may be bid
32 One of the "10 Attic orators"

39 Tate ___ (London art gallery)
41 Team that won the first A.F.L. championship
45 1981 Literature Nobelist Canetti
46 Stocking stuffer
47 Fabric with the same name as a Scottish river
49 French district that lent its name to a foodstuff
50 "Fantastic!"
51 Ne plus ultra
52 Work within a company, say
53 Density symbol, in physics
54 Material at the basis of "Jurassic Park"

by Patrick Berry

ACROSS
1 Be an agent of
7 Shock source, sometimes
15 Hawaiian "thank you"
16 Exchange for something you really want?
17 Handle, e.g.
18 Catholic
19 Wrestler Flair
20 They might just squeak by in a basketball game
22 Grooming brand introduced in 1977
24 Runners with hoods
25 Sound from a silencer
28 1965 Sonny Bono hit
31 "Berenice" author, briefly
33 Constellation seen on the flags of Australia, Samoa and Papua New Guinea
35 Club's cover
37 "___ Peak" (1997 Pierce Brosnan film)
38 Parliamentary address?
42 This, in Thüringen
43 Striking figures
46 Regulation targets for Theodore Roosevelt: Abbr.
47 "Deal with it!"
49 Catchers of some ring leaders
50 Hard up
53 Seraglio section
54 Void
57 Second chance

59 Opposite of diminish
60 "Let's have it"
61 Cardinals' gathering place
62 Violent

DOWN
1 Unscrupulous
2 Pantheon heads?
3 Fights with knights
4 Cool, in a way
5 Hockey player Tverdovsky
6 Youngest of the Culkin brothers
7 Gather
8 Scale developer
9 One-room house, typically
10 Skin pics?
11 Truncation indications: Abbr.

12 Skin pic?
13 Agent Gold on HBO's "Entourage"
14 It has pickup lines
21 It has many functions
23 Ancient meeting places
25 Cleaning product that may be useful after a party
26 Spray source
27 Amoco alternative
29 Short, close-fitting jacket
30 To ___
32 Desert Storm reporter
34 Home of Theo. Roosevelt Natl. Park
35 U.S.N. position
36 Eyebrow makeup

39 Speak explosively in anger
40 Dumps
41 Come back
44 Tree with double-toothed leaves and durable wood
45 Bad-tempered
48 Give a stemwinder
50 Bygone magistrate
51 Even ___
52 Lexicographic concern
54 "I get it" responses
55 See, say
56 Turbulent water stretch
58 Tribe visited by Lewis and Clark

by Paula Gamache

ACROSS

1 Visits
8 French sentry's cry
15 Enter quickly
16 Ethically indifferent
17 "Again . . ."
18 With intensity
19 Four quarters, in France
20 Atlas sect.
22 Yugoslavian-born court star
23 Chuck
24 Purely physical
26 Show some spunk
27 Court
28 Curl tightly
30 When Hölle freezes over?
31 Pro sports team that moved from New Orleans in 1979
33 Shakes
35 Fat cat
37 Make tracks
40 Concavo-convex lens
44 UV index monitor
45 If it's regular, each of its angles is 144°
47 "Notorious" film studio
48 Memphis's locale
50 Grandparent, frequently
51 One raised on a farm
52 Some jackets
54 Philip of "Kung Fu"
55 Schwarzenegger title role
56 Outerwear fabric
58 Ding Dong alternative
60 Umm al-Quwain, for one
61 Pro Football Hall-of-Famer-turned-congressman Steve
62 Lured
63 Hides from the enemy, say

DOWN

1 Type of massage
2 Not removed delicately
3 Porthole view
4 The singing voice, informally
5 Old sticker
6 Overseas "-ess"
7 Authenticate, in a way
8 Tiger's-eye, essentially
9 Short family member?
10 "___ in the Morning"
11 Helped someone get a seat
12 Mayo's place
13 1974 Best Actress nominee Perrine
14 Champs ___
21 Approach to arithmetic that emphasizes underlying ideas rather than exact calculations
24 Not generic
25 Daughter of Ferdinand III
28 Greenland's Scoresby Sound is the world's longest
29 Classic American watchmaker
32 Insurance letters
34 Abbr. before many state names
36 "Go easy, please"
37 Had a problem with one's suits?
38 Model
39 Kind of intake
41 Got started, with "up"
42 Locale of the Carpathian Mountains, in part
43 "The New Colossus" and the like
46 Blarneyed
49 When most Capricornios are born
51 One beaten by a beatnik
53 Not split
55 No. of People?
57 A season abroad
59 Showing fatigue

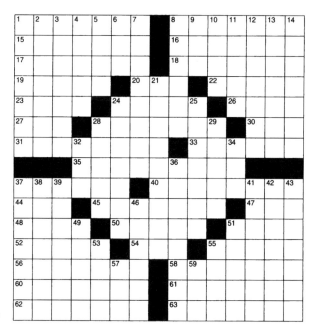

by Barry C. Silk

ACROSS

1 What you might do at the beach
10 Lethargy
15 Early inhabitant
16 Light smoke
17 Choked up
18 This is a test
19 Shaw who led the Gramercy Five
20 Muscleman with a 1980s cartoon series
21 Old-time actress Crabtree
22 Subject of interest in the question "Who are you wearing?"
23 Modern-day monarch, for short
24 Register
25 Brian known for 33-Across music
26 John who succeeded Pierre Trudeau as Canadian P.M.
28 Uris hero
29 Comment after getting something
30 Waves with long wavelengths?
33 See 25-Across
37 "Ash Wednesday" writer
38 Starry-eyed
40 Movie villain voiced by Douglas Rain
41 Miss ___
42 Spell checker?
44 Indian viceroy's authority
47 Damascus V.I.P.
50 Eventful times
51 "Take ___ the River" (Talking Heads hit)
52 Geometric prefix
53 Kip spender
54 Spanish kitties
55 Jerk
56 Doesn't support a conspiracy theory?

58 Deleted part
59 Oslo Accords concern
60 Gear
61 Frank Zappa or Dizzy Gillespie feature

DOWN

1 Forced feeding, as with a tube
2 Moon of Uranus named for a Shakespearean character
3 Like a romantic dinner
4 Big name in pest control
5 Get to
6 Jazz ___
7 Certain switch
8 Available

9 Small in the biggest way?
10 100 to 1, e.g.
11 Actress Nancy of "Sunset Boulevard"
12 Sandwich filler
13 Church piece
14 Old Tory
23 Fundamental energy units
26 "Vincent & ___" (1990 Robert Altman film)
27 Dailies, in the movie biz
29 ___-en-Provence, France
31 Groomed
32 Word before and after "in"
33 Swimming, surfboarding, etc.
34 Uncombed

35 Whitewall, maybe
36 Delays
39 Largest of the ABC islands
43 "The Tao that can be told is not the eternal Tao" philosopher
44 "Touché!" elicitor
45 Not accented
46 Important figure in the Gospels
48 Faulkner's "___ for Emily"
49 Out
51 1945 conference site for Roosevelt and Churchill
54 One might fight to the last one
57 Sonny's partner in "Dog Day Afternoon"

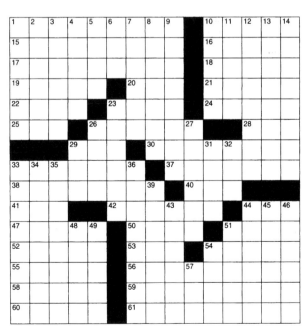

by John Farmer

ACROSS

1 Just the pits
16 Classic line of debate?
17 Just a bit, if that
18 Flag holder
19 In shape
20 Means: Abbr.
21 Songwriter Coleman and others
22 Illumination indication
23 Food whose name means "little sash"
28 Many an e-mail attachment
30 Sewn up
37 "The Randi Rhodes Show" network
38 Determine
39 It'll change your mind
40 Drone
41 Dance move
44 Scratch
46 Winner of three consecutive Emmys for "Mission: Impossible"
47 Batman creator Bob
49 Woody Guthrie's "Tom ___"
53 Left-of-center party member
57 "I'll take whatever help I can get"
58 Pro team whose mascot is a blue bird named Blitz

DOWN

1 Thrashers' home in the N.H.L.: Abbr.
2 One just filling up space
3 Second of 24
4 See 52-Down
5 Arm raiser, informally
6 Vote for
7 In need of a sweep
8 Ragged edges, in metalworking
9 Lambs: Lat.
10 Destiny
11 String player?
12 Ottoman officers
13 Simple
14 Toot
15 Some specialize in elec.
21 They may give you a seat
22 Spring river phenomenon
23 Soundproofing material
24 Converse alternative
25 Yo-yo
26 Requiem title word
27 Alternative to a 23-Across
28 Somewhat, in music
29 Embarrassing way to be caught
31 1856 antislavery novel
32 Insult, on the street
33 Volt-ampere
34 Peculiar: Prefix
35 Relative of -ance
36 Perfect
41 He wrote that government "is but a necessary evil"
42 Gulf of Sidra setting
43 Like the Keystone Kops
44 "The ___ near!"
45 New Hampshire's ___ State College
46 Longfellow's "The Bells of San ___"
47 Rove in politics
48 Old man, in Mannheim
49 Rib
50 Prefix with -hedron
51 In ranks
52 With 4-Down, black magic
54 Raise a stink?
55 Billy's call
56 Logos and the like: Abbr.

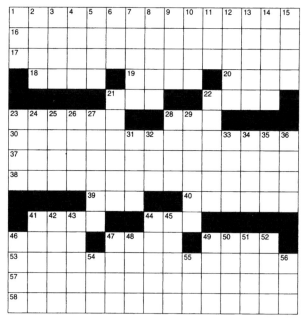

by Paula Gamache

ACROSS

1 Doesn't sit well
16 Class in which various schools are discussed
17 One way to solve problems
18 Pacer maker: Abbr.
19 Red sky, perhaps
20 "___ dispraise my lord . . .": Juliet
21 Expert in ancient law
24 City on the Natchez Trace
26 Not backing, in the backwoods
27 Lengthens, old-style
31 Retiree's coverage?
32 Basis for a suit
33 "30 Rock" creator
35 What a future American might take: Abbr.
36 Didn't paw
37 ___ grecque
40 Balloon attachment
41 Object in a Monet painting
42 Member of la famille immédiate
45 Floors
46 Frauen, across the border: Abbr.
47 Least spotted
49 Front wheel divergence
51 Hacker's cry of success
52 Something needed for your sake?
56 Gouge, say
57 Daydreaming, e.g.

62 Completely gone
63 Records of interest to real estate agents

DOWN

1 Distillation location
2 Suffix with cream
3 Encouraging remark
4 Predatory critter
5 Large accounts?
6 Place for jets
7 1968 folk album
8 Bit of moonshine
9 Adolescent outburst
10 Louis Armstrong's "Oh ___ He Ramble"
11 Initials of a noted "Wizard"
12 Go downhill
13 No follower

14 Drive along leisurely
15 Firmly establish
21 Like some shifts
22 Occasional clashers
23 Dakota tongue
25 ___ to be
28 Rather informal?
29 Help set up chairs for?
30 French study, e.g.
34 Take many courses
36 They're against each other
37 Relating to heraldry
38 Place
39 Kind of producer: Abbr.
40 It may contain tear gas

41 Emphatic turndown
42 Curly-haired "Peanuts" character
43 20th-dynasty ruler
44 Lois Lane player Durance and others
48 It may be wrapped in a bun
50 Astrologer with the autobiography "Answer in the Sky"
53 Iraq's ___ Ali Shrine
54 Grant
55 Business class, briefly
58 Hearing aids, for short
59 Now in
60 R.S.V.P. component
61 D.C. United org.

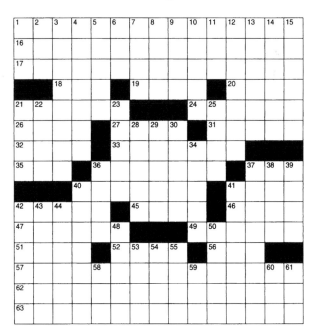

by Harvey Estes

ACROSS
1 Navigation hazard
9 Coolness
15 Way off
16 Special delivery?
17 Married man who had long been a bachelor
18 Many a monthly check writer
19 Missing the point?
21 Car bar
22 W.W. II agcy.
23 Drawer units?
25 ___ Genevieve County, Mo.
26 Take off
29 When repeated, a "Funny Girl" song
30 Utterance when pointing to a woman
31 Chief
32 Famously fussy pair of diners
33 Any of les Trois Mousquetaires
34 Acts on a gut feeling?
35 Gold rush storyteller
36 Hardware store offering
37 In the style of: Suffix
38 Fishing boats
39 Island republic
40 ___ phenomenon (optical illusion)
41 Like most mammals
42 He wrote "A first sign of the beginning of understanding is the wish to die"
43 Top of some scales
44 Chump
45 Univ. offerings
46 Not having as favorable a prognosis

48 Main, maybe
53 Quiet craft
55 Dangerous places for correspondents
56 Bunny backer?
57 Where workers gather
58 Risers meet them
59 QB who was the 1963 N.F.L. M.V.P.

DOWN
1 Five-time U.S. presidential candidate in the early 1900s
2 One making firm decisions
3 Hombre, once
4 Some athletes shoot them
5 Like many an heir apparent
6 Goes under
7 If ever
8 Overdoes it
9 Not out of place
10 Importunes
11 Carnival follower
12 "Che!" title role player, 1969
13 Watch notch
14 Alternative that should be followed
20 Put under?
24 The Chi-___ (1970s R & B group)
26 "Pleasant dreams"
27 Seed-separating gizmo
28 Past prime time?
29 U.S. air-to-air missile
32 Navigation hazard
36 "C'mon, do me this favor"
38 Ordained
42 Post-Taliban Afghan president
45 Kind of scholarship
47 Mrs. Turnblad in "Hairspray"
49 Spanish hors d'oeuvre
50 Competing
51 Strip
52 Forum infinitive
54 Commuters' choices: Abbr.

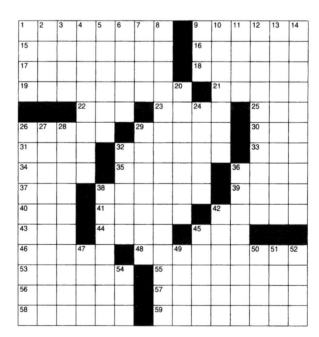

by Lynn Lempel

ACROSS
1 Stuck
8 "Not possible"
14 It might go off during a 30-Across
16 "Great taste since 1905" sloganeer
17 Rule broken in leisure?
18 He died soon after escaping from Crete
19 ___ dog
20 Dutch export
22 Van Halen's "Live Without ___"
23 Angle iron
24 TV series whose finale was titled "The Truth," with "The"
26 Unpleasant thing to incur
27 Squadron leader?
28 Swear words?
30 One can be tracked
31 2000 Olympics host
32 Recurring character who dies in the novel "Curtain"
34 Reveals
35 Dusting aid
36 Unesco World Heritage Site on the Arabian Peninsula
37 Scheduled
39 Letters on some college buildings
42 A.L. Central scoreboard abbr.
43 Little tricksters
44 Having good balance
45 Target of milk of magnesia
47 Informal demurral
48 Has a problem on the road

49 College in Claremont, Calif.
51 Tax burden?
53 It might go 7-5
54 Thing with a pressure point?
55 Grinder
56 Butterfly feature

DOWN
1 Totally unemotional type
2 Wheels
3 Things with rings
4 Further out of the woods?
5 Trick
6 One making waves
7 Kids' hideaway
8 Where many prints may be found

9 10-Down div.
10 Org. since 1910
11 Raked over the coals
12 Horse of a certain color
13 Occasions for baskets
15 Clairvoyant
21 Substitute: Abbr.
24 Abscissa
25 Barraged
28 "A Prairie Home Companion" co-star, 2006
29 "Odyssey" high point
30 "Star Wars" order
32 Fruit found among needles

33 Routinely
34 Battle of Put-in-Bay setting
35 16-Across, e.g.
36 General who prevailed over Carthage
38 Big name in ergonomic utensils
39 Settled
40 Shade deeper than heliotrope
41 Sonnet section
44 Flying predators of cold seas
46 "O mighty Caesar! ___ thou lie so low?": Shak.
48 Learned
50 "Tutte ___ cor vi sento" (Mozart aria)
52 ___ dog

by Mike Nothnagel

ACROSS

1 Windshield wipers
10 "Unbelievable!"
15 Darwin's home
16 Superrealist sculptor Hanson
17 Zip
18 They stand for something: Abbr.
19 Station info, briefly
20 Checks out
21 1984 hit parody of a 1983 hit song
22 Get moving, with "up"
23 Four-time Vardon Trophy winner
25 Area below the hairline
26 Lock changer?
29 Turn out
31 Narrows: Abbr.
32 Directory data: Abbr.
34 Clam
36 Bluster
40 Hardly humble homes
41 A bit much
43 Call in a calamity
44 No longer doing the job?: Abbr.
45 Bombards with junk
47 Become active
50 Pull out of ___ (produce suddenly)
52 Makes out
54 Fat cat, in England
56 Packs in stacks
58 Short distance
59 "Eight Is Enough" wife

60 Creator of lofty lines
61 Freshening naturally
63 Something to get a kick out of
64 Park gathering place
65 Starters
66 Garb symbolizing youth

DOWN

1 Not as touched
2 Like successful orators
3 James Forrestal was its last cabinet secy.
4 Portions of les années
5 Stat for a reliever
6 Slalom targets
7 Comic Boosler
8 Astronaut Collins and others
9 Toasted triangle topper
10 One of Jon Arbuckle's pets
11 Changsha is its capital
12 "Hang on!"
13 Eager
14 Things that may be shot in stages?
24 "La Reine Margot" novelist
27 ___'acte
28 Ways to go
30 Some shirts
33 Dishes out undaintily

35 Trailer's place
36 South Pacific island
37 Cry before storming out
38 "Lighten up, will ya?!"
39 Hiking aid
42 Hate, say
46 "Tristram Shandy" author
48 Natural
49 In the pink
51 10 kilogauss
53 Relish
55 Disk units
57 Bring to a standstill
59 Mar makeup
62 Letter run

by Frederick J. Healy

ACROSS

1 News Corporation-owned Web site that's one of the 10 most visited sites in the world
8 Dirt on a person
14 Yellow fliers with large eyespots
15 "Cab," e.g.
16 Abscond
17 What the key of D minor has
18 Sponge
19 Driving distance is a concern in it
21 Dermal opening?
22 Miss Gulch biter
24 Height and such
25 Pet
26 Hostile
28 In advance of
29 Get a handle on?
30 They're played at the track
32 Buries
34 Brass
36 Walled city of the Mideast
37 "Let me live my own life!"
41 Gives a little, say
45 Wedding concern
46 Taper
48 Was sluggish?
49 Old Testament book: Abbr.
50 Reporting to
52 Vapid
53 1980s sitcom title role
54 Flips
56 Hiver's opposite
57 Not-so-good feeling
59 Former field food
61 Terminal timesaver

62 Its value is in creasing
63 Sprint acquisition of 2005
64 Crossword source since 1942: Abbr.

DOWN

1 Slip
2 Poem reader at the 2006 Olympics opening ceremony
3 Gaga
4 With 20-Down, waffle alternative
5 Capping
6 Finishes quickly, in a way
7 Groundskeeper's charge
8 Family group
9 ___-Neisse Line
10 Abbr. in personal ads
11 Center of Connecticut
12 All thrown together, say
13 Little women
15 Cheering section
20 See 4-Down
23 "Heavens!"
25 1963 Academy Awards host
27 He wrote "It's certain that fine women eat / A crazy salad with their meat"
29 Alb coverer
31 Sharp
33 Meal source
35 Lopsided court result
37 Ones paid to conceive?

38 Cartoon boss working at a quarry
39 Modern rental option
40 Sch. whose colors are "true blue" and gold
42 Cry upon arriving
43 Beau ideal
44 Burial place of many French kings
47 "Way to go, dude!"
50 Bernoulli family birthplace
51 Trouble
54 Raise
55 Not yet 58-Down
58 See 55-Down
60 ___ Friday's

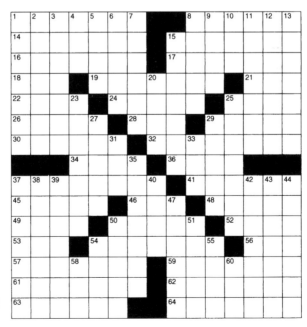

by David Quarfoot

ACROSS

1 He had a hit with "The Joint Is Jumpin' "
11 Signs of neglect
15 First #1 hit by the Beach Boys
16 Like the sea
17 City on the Transcontinental Railroad
18 Some people have it for life
19 Not do the rite thing?
20 Requests for developers: Abbr.
21 Taylor of "Mystic Pizza"
22 Some cabbage
23 Dwell
24 Much
25 With 52- and 39-Across, gradually
26 Potentate
28 One of a primer pair
29 They're not originals
31 Materials used as inert paint fillers
33 Best people
34 El relative
35 Whole slew of
39 See 25-Across
43 Premium chargers, briefly
44 Like a well-maintained lawn
46 Discriminatory leader?
47 What "y" might become
48 Driver on a ranch
49 It's found in a chest
50 Fermentation locations
52 See 25-Across
53 19th-century territorial capital
54 Organs are located in it: Abbr.
55 Block head?
57 Delivery possibility
58 Committed a sports no-no
59 Due and sei
60 Succulent African shrub popular as a bonsai

DOWN

1 Internet Explorer alternative
2 Facial feature, later in life
3 Carpenter, at times
4 They're located on organs
5 Draw to a close
6 It may come after you
7 Hippie happenings
8 African city of 2.5+ million founded by the Portuguese
9 Infinite
10 Food figs.
11 Hanging setting
12 Big name in credit reports
13 Greyhounds may run in it
14 Wilde things?
23 "See ya!"
26 Year of St. Genevieve's death
27 Pitching
28 Fun
30 They're known for head-turning
32 Basketful
35 Fictional doctor
36 "This is no joke!"
37 Letter writing, some say
38 It was first observed in 1846
39 One taken in
40 Like some surgery
41 Group that starred in the 1968 film "Head," with "the"
42 Match-starting cry
45 Establishes
49 Challenge for a shortstop
51 Target of heavy W.W. II bombing, 1944
52 "That ___ . . ."
53 Comfortable
56 Discount designation: Abbr.

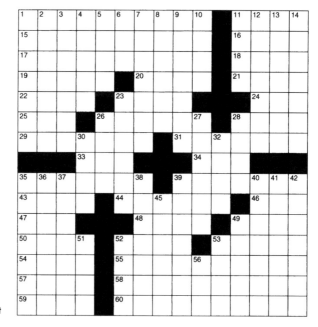

by Barry C. Silk

ACROSS
1 Concerned query
6 Without a leg to stand on?
14 Vermont senator Sanders
15 It's a cinch
16 Pretentious
17 Without a match
18 "Pardon me"
19 Closing bid?
20 Peak
21 McCartney, to fans
24 Horror film that starts in a filthy lavatory
26 Weaken, in a way
29 Monotheistic Syrian
33 Most in need of toning
35 Top-rated, in a way
36 Slant
37 Get all histrionic
38 About 40 degrees, for N.Y.C.
39 Hostel environments
40 Wore out
42 Some lap dogs
44 Result of a new TV series' renewal
46 A.A. discussion topic
48 Appoints as an agent
49 Roast pig side dish
52 Stands
55 Brew choice
56 Afro-Caribbean religion
58 Toeless creature in an Edward Lear verse
60 Engine manufacturer Briggs & ___
61 One with a second helping
62 Super Bowl XX champs
63 Personnel director, at times

DOWN
1 Hoped-for reply to 1-Across
2 Payment is often sent with one
3 Apt to say "So?"
4 Relative of -ish
5 Mauna ___
6 Missile with a mobile launcher
7 Product whose ads featured twins
8 Iroquois' foes
9 Lee Marvin TV oldie
10 Moldovan money
11 He or I, but not you: Abbr.
12 Ward of "Once and Again"
13 Deep river?
14 Sighing a lot, maybe
19 Some Nissans
22 "___ for Alibi"
23 ___ Pendragon, King Arthur's father
25 Call slip?
27 West African currency
28 Ponch player in 1970s–'80s TV
30 Too awful even to fix up, as an apartment
31 Octopus, e.g.
32 Take the cake?
34 Twit
36 Marcel Marceau character
41 Bush league?
43 City connected to the 4.1-mile long Sunshine Skyway Br.
45 Kitchen appliance brand
47 In a sense
49 "Over here"
50 Four-letter word, aptly
51 On
53 Pricey gown
54 McShane and McKellen
57 Bill
58 Sharable computer file, for short
59 Overseas agreement

by Henry Hook

ACROSS

1 "That may be true, but . . ."
11 ". . . there are evils ___ to darken all his goodness": Shak.
15 Visit
16 ___ Lemaris, early love of Superman
17 When a procrastinator tends to something
18 Exultant cry
19 Advance further?
20 Comic Boosler
22 Place of refuge
26 Tons of fun
27 It's built for a trial
31 Shot putters' supplies?
33 Player of June in "Henry & June"
34 Title locale of five 1980s films: Abbr.
36 Russian peasant wear
38 Chic
40 No-nonsense cry
41 King's second
43 Diamond, e.g.
44 Like petty offs.
45 She had brief roles as Phyllis on "Rhoda" and Rhoda on "Dr. Kildare"
47 Prize cup, maybe
48 Jazz pianist who played with Satchmo
50 Address south of the border
52 They're thick
54 Feast
59 Ones going head to head
60 Magazine that hands out annual Independent Press Awards
64 Part of a rebel name
65 Little redhead
66 "Buona ___!"
67 Puppet glue-ons

DOWN

1 Alexis, e.g.
2 Improve
3 Green's concern: Abbr.
4 Italian tenor ___ Schipa
5 Routine responses?
6 Soap actress Kristen and others
7 Money machine mfr.
8 Knock around
9 Pier grp.
10 Roy Rogers's surname at birth
11 Son of Elam whose name means "God the Lord"
12 Response to "I had no idea!"
13 Northeastern city named for a Penobscot chief
14 One concerned with the nose
21 Some of those who "hail the new" in "Deck the Halls"
23 Arrow of Light earner's program
24 Nostalgia elicitor
25 Cry "nyah, nyah!"
27 Engagement breakers?
28 Outlaw band member
29 Insignificant sort
30 Saki story whose title character is a hyena
32 Clammed up
35 Felix, e.g.
37 Bête noire
39 Modern provider of fast service, briefly
42 Nugget holder
46 Light reddish-brown
49 God commanded him to marry a harlot
51 Like some instruments
53 Like some instruments: Abbr.
55 "What's Going On" singer, 1971
56 What you may call it when you're wiped out
57 New Wave singer Lovich
58 Shore scavengers
61 Governing creative principle
62 Vietnam's ___ Dinh Diem
63 It's most useful when cracked

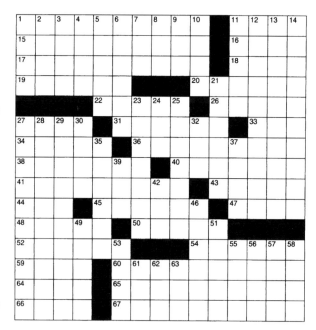

by Myles Callum

ACROSS

1 Backup
6 Squirts
10 Size in a lingerie shop
14 Music maker "played" by the wind
16 Basse-Normandie department
17 Stereotypical nerd
18 2004–06 poet laureate Kooser and others
19 Boards
20 Fluffy, perhaps
22 Tears
24 Trainee
25 Zodiac symbol
28 ___ Britannica
29 Navajo handicrafts
31 Car rental company founder Warren
33 Country with coups d'état in 2000 and 2006
35 Airline purchased by T.W.A. in 1986
36 Cellist who debuted at London's Wigmore Hall at age 16
39 Invite to one's penthouse suite
40 Robed dignitary
41 Fen bender
42 Availed
44 It lands at Landvetter
46 Holders of shoulders: Abbr.
47 Ancient Greek sculptor famous for his athletes in bronze
48 Inclusive pronoun
50 Cautious people stay on it
52 Shakespearean scholar Edmond
56 Problem ending
57 Expensive choice for a commuter
59 Big name in contact lens cleaners
60 "Madame Butterfly," updated
61 Peer on a stage
62 Being tossed, maybe
63 Statistical calculations

DOWN

1 Tio ___ (sherry brand)
2 Crazy
3 Set down
4 Bronc rival
5 Wrongful slammer sentence, say
6 Appreciation abbreviation
7 Curses
8 Palm smartphone
9 Smart
10 Fashionable resort area
11 Piñata decoration
12 Not put off
13 Raid victim
15 Instant success?
21 Indian lute
23 Like Shakespeare's Prospero, e.g.
25 Javanese chiefs
26 Salt halter
27 It'll knock you out after you knock it back
29 1996 Golden Globe winner for "Truman"
30 Variety listings
32 Like some diamonds
34 Lord of fiction
37 Beehives, e.g.
38 He wrote "In the country of the blind the one-eyed man is king"
43 Knot
45 Gomer Pyle expletive
48 Where the Fulda flows
49 Cartoonist Segar
50 Pioneering puppeteer
51 Place of honor
53 Grammy-winning merengue singer Tañón
54 Rialto sign
55 Coastal avifauna
58 Fed. property overseer

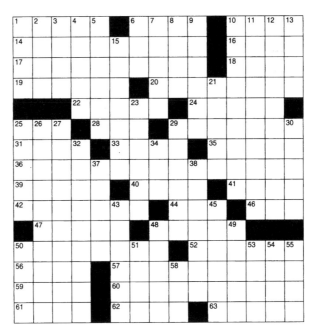

by Karen M. Tracey

ACROSS

1 African city with famed botanical gardens
8 Riddle ender
15 Yosemite setting
16 Still oblivious
17 It has a fast, easy gait
19 Things you enjoy doing
20 Having new tournament rankings
21 Marxist quality?
29 Dish with tomato sauce
36 Area of W.W. II fighting
37 Like Dacron
38 Pros
39 Football helmet features
47 One working for a flat fee?
54 Has an accommodating spirit
55 Island just north of the Equator
56 Advances
57 Activity of an organism in response to light, e.g.
58 Puts away

DOWN

1 Spanish 101 verb
2 Wedding invitee
3 Wedding rentals
4 ___ Davis, first African-American to win the Heisman Trophy
5 Music symbol
6 Set (in)
7 "Ah, Wilderness!" mother

8 PBS station behind Charlie Rose
9 British general in the American Revolution
10 "I'll raise the preparation of ___": Mark Antony
11 Square in a steam room
12 Bids
13 A runner might enter it
14 Some flawed mdse.
18 Spot from which you might see a bomb headed your way
22 Recipe details: Abbr.
23 Cadbury Schweppes brand

24 Composition of some French chains
25 Drink preference
26 Editorial cartoonist Hulme
27 Antique gun
28 Harvard Science Center architect José Luis ___
29 Dry, in Durango
30 Reverse movement, of a sort
31 Cézanne's "Boy in ___ Vest"
32 Longtime "All Things Considered" host Adams
33 Itself, in a Latin legal phrase
34 Not secret
35 Compact

40 Things hypothesized by Democritus
41 Move shoots, say
42 Flaky Turkish confection
43 Some moldings
44 Canine line
45 Follow
46 Way down
47 Popular U.S. board game since 1959
48 He played Bob in "La Bamba," 1987
49 It goes on and on and on
50 Former
51 They're big in Hollywood
52 Rest stop sight
53 "___ Hombres" (ZZ Top record)

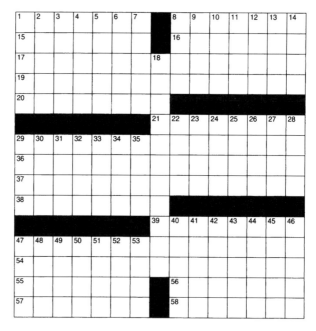

by Brendan Emmett Quigley

ACROSS

1 Interest of Miss Marple
5 Blow-drying problem
15 Liner's locale
16 Slipping frequencies
17 Spot
18 Steering system components
19 "___ the glad waters of the dark blue sea": Byron
20 James Bond was kicked out of it
21 Eric of "Lucky You"
22 Contortionist's inspiration?
24 Aquavit flavorer
27 Risible
28 Paris fashion house since 1956
29 Seed's exterior
30 Off by a mile
34 1990s Indian P.M.
35 Where some addresses come from
36 Massenet's "Le ___ de Lahore"
37 Setting of Camus's "The Fall"
40 One yawning
42 Sign at some booths
43 Marina accommodations
44 Notoriety
47 Hansom cab accessory
48 Massive star
49 Half of doce
50 Something often smelled
51 Factor in a home's market value
55 Do groundbreaking work?
56 Carried by currents, in a way
57 Winetaster's concern
58 Serenity
59 Forum infinitive

DOWN

1 Shakespearean character who introduced the phrase "salad days"
2 Tattoo remover
3 Coffeehouse menu subheading
4 1959 #1 Frankie Avalon hit
5 Tested, as a load
6 Documentarian Morris
7 Elvis follower
8 Lot
9 Richard Gere title role of 2000
10 Basso Berberian
11 Sports champ depicted in "Cinderella Man," 2005
12 Counselor-___
13 Davis of "Cutthroat Island"
14 Theme
20 Fitch who co-founded Abercrombie & Fitch
23 Indication of disapproval
24 Novelist Potok
25 Tony winner for "Guys and Dolls," 1951
26 Detail on some tickets
28 Material used in making saunas
30 "Pink Shoe Laces" singer Stevens
31 "Elijah" and others
32 Bridle parts
33 Piercing glance
35 Coventry park sight
38 It's raised after a payment is collected
39 Disney doe
40 Pinches
41 Part of a laugh
43 Temporary property holder
44 Konica Minolta competitor
45 Elicit
46 Chick playing a piano
47 Isn't quite neutral
49 Toxin fighters
52 Symbol of industry
53 "Be more . . ." sloganeer
54 "Some Words With a Mummy" penner
55 Honourary title: Abbr.

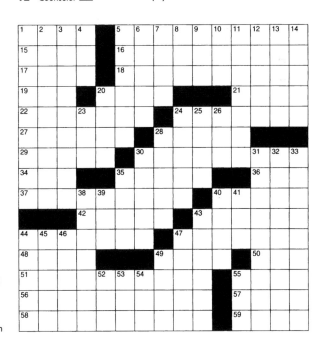

by Brad Wilber

ACROSS

1 Mad magazine feature
9 Spherical bacteria
14 Weekly since 1865
16 Financial V.I.P.
17 Martin of Hollywood
18 Quaint contraction
19 Puts in
20 Admits
22 Falls apart
23 Not quite up yet
24 Pick apart
25 1990s N.F.L. running back Curtis ___
26 ___ Paradise of Kerouac's "On the Road"
27 Keep in order
29 Ones needing fulfillment?
30 Locale for most of the New York Marathon
32 Kind of state
33 Rest stops?
36 Dobby or Winky, in Harry Potter
39 Solo
40 Hum follower?
41 "Pinocchio" character voiced by Mel Blanc
42 "That hurts!"
43 Played out
45 Rialto Bridge sight
46 One use for anise
48 Risqué
49 Not broadside
50 Mountain climber's need
52 Jaguar maker
53 When Hamlet first sees a ghost

54 Band active from 1995 to 2002
55 Providers of peer review?

DOWN

1 Figure in many jokes
2 Troop group
3 Arabs who are not in OPEC
4 Some sweaters
5 Smelling things
6 London's Covent Garden and others: Abbr.
7 Dicks
8 Daredevil's creed
9 Home of "The NFL Today"
10 Bishop Museum setting
11 Small sunfish
12 Help for a secret agent
13 Cantillates
15 1995 political book subtitled "Leader of the Second American Revolution"
21 When the kids are out
23 Old drive-in fare
26 "Happy Days" catchphrase
28 The General ___, "The Dukes of Hazzard" auto
30 Beyond oblivious
31 Turned

32 Half of a 1960s R & B duo
33 Source of lecithin
34 Chooses
35 Part of the Tribune Company
36 Current events around Christmas
37 Round steak, e.g.
38 Kind of crystals
41 Wine order
44 Rounds: Abbr.
45 Addition sign
47 It's hard to walk on
48 Rise by the shore
51 "The Partridge Family" actress

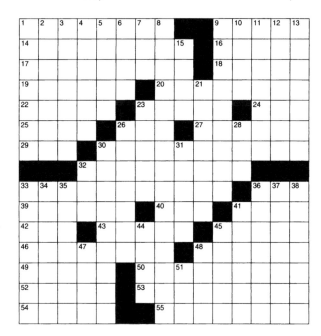

by Mark Diehl

ACROSS

1 When
9 Slip covers?
15 She was executed in 1917
16 100 centésimos
17 "Nonsense!"
19 Pentax Spotmatic, e.g., in brief
20 Boy in the comic strip "Rose Is Rose"
21 Parents
22 Parts of many jam sessions
25 Minute
27 African evergreen shrub
29 Vlasic varieties
30 Get ready to grill
33 Like VCRs in the 1970s
36 Delicacy
39 One-striper: Abbr.
40 Stuck with no way out
41 Kitchen pieces
43 Animal visitor to Paris in a classic children's book
44 Cornmeal concoction
47 One that takes a picture?
49 Crosses
50 Lead, e.g.
52 Engraved message?: Abbr.
55 "I'm not volunteering!"
59 Ring of anatomy
60 Boring people
61 On notice
62 "Tonka" star, 1958

DOWN

1 Withdrawal figs.
2 Joke writer for many Kennedy campaign speeches
3 Astrological set
4 Some husk contents
5 Understanding responses
6 Pusher
7 Botanical appendages
8 Fries, say
9 A telly may get it
10 Old Olympics award
11 Scarlett O'Hara's mother and others
12 W.W. II vessel
13 Cascades
14 Flip
18 Comment before turning in
23 Director of the Associated Press, 1900–35
24 Scale succession
26 Nicholas Gage title character
27 More
28 Tout's opposite
29 45-Down performers
31 How some hats are worn
32 Drawing, e.g.
33 Start of some countdowns
34 "Piece of My Heart" singer Franklin
35 Result of regular use
37 "Sin City" actress, 2005
38 Stagecoach puller
41 Body band
42 Flat part
44 17-Across, quaintly
45 See 29-Down
46 Parfait part
47 It's a big part of life
48 Do some tune-up work on
51 Aurora producer
53 2002 Literature Nobelist Kertész
54 Capital of Colombia
56 Land of "20,000 Leagues Under the Sea"
57 Dutch traveler's choice
58 Figure in the Sunni/Shia split

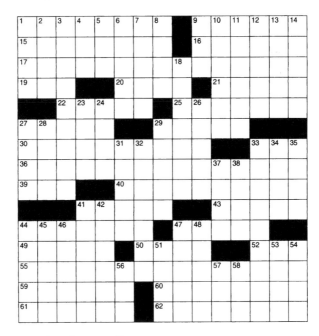

by Robert H. Wolfe

ACROSS

1 Blockbuster alternative
8 Material for drainage lines
15 Just as anyone can be
16 What some bombs release
17 Early filmmaking brothers Auguste and Louis ___
18 What a cause might turn into
19 Noted 1915 West Point grad.
20 Bond type whose first purchaser was F.D.R.
22 Atkins diet no-no
23 "No god but God" author ___ Aslan
25 ___ Malfoy, bully in Harry Potter books
26 German city where Napoleon defeated the Prussians
27 States
29 Org. with a Council on Ethical and Judicial Affairs
30 Pitch problems?
31 May day events, perhaps
33 Big name in coffee makers
35 Ruffles
37 "Oh, I give up!"
41 Rot
43 Minus sign equivalent
44 Fractional currency
47 A sucker, for short
49 Layered dessert
50 Reunion gatherers
51 Apollo's birthplace
53 Be reminiscent of
54 Part of "the many," in Greek
55 Scull part
57 Printed

58 Noted Art Deco building in the Big Apple, with "the"
60 Dinar spender
62 Some
63 1962 hit with the lyric "Like the samba sound, my heart begins to pound"
64 Shop tool with pulleys
65 Has at a spread

DOWN

1 Annual sports event with seven rounds
2 Brandy
3 Mountain, e.g.
4 What many workers look forward to: Abbr.
5 Refuse
6 "The East ___" (1960s Chinese anthem)

7 Nissan model
8 Track warm-up leaders
9 Back of a leaf
10 "Red, White & ___" (2005 rock album)
11 On the plus side?: Abbr.
12 Deadly 2003 hurricane that hit North Carolina
13 It's far from a metropolis
14 Figure skater Sokolova and others
21 Foot type
24 Totally covered by
26 Miss No-Name
28 Relative of a cutter
30 Black, say
32 Hub NW of LAX
34 Buddy, in slang

36 Plant used as an herbal remedy for headaches
38 Rallying slogans
39 "Who'd a thunk it?!"
40 Paper that calls itself "America's Finest News Source"
42 Dialectal contraction
44 Brokerage giant
45 Zoological cavity
46 Criticize harshly and repeatedly
48 Like some books
51 Friend of Porky
52 "Pardon me," in Parma
55 Dropping sound
56 Tae ___ do
59 Bomb not bursting in air?
61 Bart Simpson's grandpa

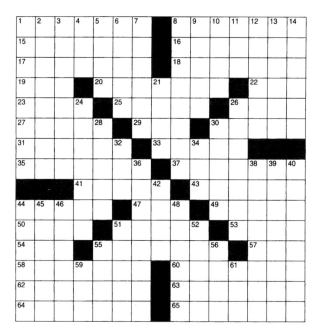

by Brendan Emmett Quigley and David Quarfoot

ACROSS

1 Classic sports lineup
11 All in favor
15 Antipathy
16 Not be fair?
17 "I hear ya!"
18 Regard impolitely
19 Low square
20 Work period
21 Intelligence problem
22 Winter fall, in Falkirk
23 Fortune 500 company founded in 1995
24 It's often administered orally
25 Needle holders
27 Power system
28 Birthplace of Evel Knievel and Martha Raye
29 Dill herb
30 "Follow the Fleet" co-star, 1936
32 Precursor to a historical "party"
34 Winner of four Oscars for musical scores
38 "Seems that way"
42 One-named singer with the 1960s Velvet Underground
43 Decision maker
46 Calls in a field
47 Proof word
48 Home of Gannon University
49 "I'll Be Doggone" singer, 1965
50 Lovelace who was called "The Enchantress of Numbers"
51 Cossacks' leader

52 Take the top off
54 Wild
55 Break
56 Enterprise
58 Natural healer
59 Decision maker
60 Revolutionary War general Thomas
61 Big name in foot care

DOWN

1 Dietary danger
2 Like some charms
3 Range, e.g.
4 Old character
5 Company keepers: Abbr.
6 Calendario units

7 Ribbons
8 Check
9 Preceder of many hockey games
10 Like a snood, commonly
11 Some dance honorees
12 Cousin of goulash
13 Like some old-fashioned lamps
14 Cold response?
26 1959 #1 hit for Lloyd Price
27 Track take
28 Cold response?
31 Corp. capital raisers
33 Breaking need
35 It's found in eggs

36 Like some streams in winter
37 "Isn't anyone interested?"
39 Like many supermarket lines?
40 Greet
41 Producer of some beads
43 It can give people flight reservations
44 Legendary Christian martyr
45 It's open for discussion
49 "Life Is Beautiful" hero
53 Spare change?
54 Buckling down
57 Org. with its own insurance agency

by Barry C. Silk

ACROSS

1 Small suit
7 Cheese with a greenish tint
14 "The Outsiders" author
15 Band seen at parties
16 Available if needed
17 Aircraft for the Red Baron
18 Without reservation
19 "The Blessed Damozel" poet
20 "Mr. ___," 1983 comedy
21 Military classification
23 Result of a day at the beach?
24 "Infidel" author Ayaan Hirsi ___
25 ___ Island
26 Object of Oliver Twist's request for "more"
27 Semimonthly ocean occurrence
29 Somewhat
30 "___ and Janis" (comic strip)
31 Linguist Okrand who created the Klingon language
32 It's "heavier freight for the shipper than it is for the consignee": Augustus Thomas
35 Poem whose first, third and seventh lines are identical
39 Ready to explode
40 Garçon's counterpart
41 Application file extension
42 Big seller of smoothies
43 Economist who wrote "The Theory of the Leisure Class"

44 ___-Hulk (Marvel Comics character)
45 Goshen raceway's length
47 It's cleared for a debriefing
49 In a despicable way
50 Play a flute
51 Details
52 Book before Job
53 Future hunters
54 Does a landscaper's job

DOWN

1 Troupe leader
2 Camera obscura feature
3 Laudations
4 Bibliographical abbr.
5 National chain of everything-costs-the-same stores

6 Eloise of Kay Thompson books, e.g.
7 Made an effort
8 Become evident
9 Enlivens, with "up"
10 Figure seen in a store window
11 Pan American Games participant
12 Refined
13 Author of the 2006 best seller "Culture Warrior"
15 Big step
22 Disturbance
26 Typically green tube
28 Gaffe at a social gathering, in modern lingo

29 Often-unanswered missive
31 Tough's partner
32 Seemed particularly relevant
33 Pan's realm
34 Putting aside temporarily
35 Hearty entree
36 Country of two million surrounded by a single other country
37 Let the air out, say
38 Betrays unsteadiness
40 Guys
43 See
46 Universal remote button
48 Breaks down

by Patrick Berry

ACROSS

1 Billionaire sports entrepreneur who heads HDNet
10 Like some seasonal helpers
15 Within the next few minutes, potentially
16 Some piano players
17 Case made for a shooter
18 Agitated
19 Real-estate ad statistic
20 Its motto is "All for our country": Abbr.
22 Go over
23 Orchestra section
25 Dr. Seuss's "Too Many ___"
27 Consumer protection grp.
28 Yokohama "yes"
30 Marathon runner Gebrselassie
32 It served the Mid-Atlantic until 1976
39 Classic laugh-inducing parlor game with writing or illustrations
40 Move on after a humiliating defeat
41 Claimed
42 Vintner's prefix
43 Kind of engr.
44 Member of a popular college frat
47 Parliament rival
52 Shot one on
54 Name for Quantum Computer Services since '89
55 Heavyweights compete in it
56 An overabundance
58 "You said it!"
62 Sent regrets, say
63 Help get settled
64 Priceless instrument
65 What green might ripen into

DOWN

1 Bird remarkable for its longevity
2 Breakout maker
3 Far Eastern bowlful
4 Manipulate, in a way
5 France's Saint-___-l'École
6 She played Martha in Broadway's "Who's Afraid of Virginia Woolf?"
7 One hanging around at Red Lobster?
8 Range option
9 Ben-Gurion setting
10 Stumble
11 "Happy Birthday" playwright
12 About-faces
13 Nervous
14 Band with the highest first-week album sales in music history
21 It'll get you somewhere
24 Some religious fundamentalists
25 Cook's words
26 Old settings for many out-of-tune pianos
29 Connecticut city on the Naugatuck
31 Factory seconds: Abbr.
32 Sport, for short
33 Foreignness
34 Old Spice alternative
35 Court stuff
36 Bus spec.
37 "The Mischievous Dog" author
38 ___ Peres (St. Louis suburb)
43 "Lady for a Day" director, 1933
45 One who's waited upon
46 Ecuador's southernmost coastal province
48 Provide an invitation for
49 Kind of cycle
50 Mug, e.g.
51 Cut
53 Firm part: Abbr.
57 Arms race plan: Abbr.
59 Takeaway game
60 Hot spot?
61 Gridiron datum

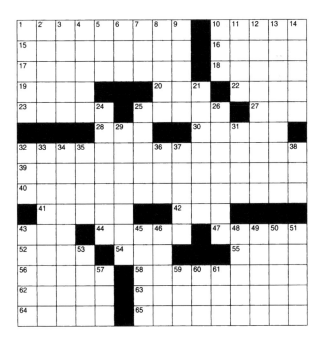

by Brendan Emmett Quigley

ACROSS

1 Sleuthing aid
11 Early education
15 Hammer wielder
16 Bangkok currency
17 YouTube phenomenon
18 ___ witness
19 Suffix with polymer
20 Walk-on parts?
21 Safari hazard
23 "Rhapsodie norvégienne" composer
24 Co-creator of Hulk and Thor
25 Napoleon, e.g.
28 Allergist's procedure
29 Lexicon listing
30 Relative of homespun
31 Century-ending Middle Ages year
32 Modern organizers, briefly
33 Judge, e.g.
34 Skittish wildlife
35 Record finish?
36 Fail to be
37 Food also called mostaccioli
38 Fictional Pulitzer-winning journalist in a 2006 film
40 Didn't fizzle
41 Aquatinting acid
42 Succeed
43 Grinders
44 One might be kidding
45 U.S.C.G. rank
48 "Madama Butterfly" wear
49 Much-anticipated Paris debut of 1992
52 Colleague of 38-Across
53 Place for trophies at an awards luncheon
54 Concert venues
55 1971 Elton John song

DOWN

1 Kind of bean
2 See 51-Down
3 Plot segment
4 Where folks go off and on: Abbr.
5 "View From the Summit" memoirist
6 Swell
7 ___ López de Loyola, founder of the Society of Jesus
8 People may get them before going to coll.
9 Part of a giggle
10 Hockey Hall-of-Famer Bryan
11 Not in the picture
12 Archer's post
13 Action thriller staple
14 Homey's acceptance
22 Innards of some clocks
23 Posts: Abbr.
24 Earth-shattering activity?
25 Casbah fugitive of French film
26 Noted diary words
27 Alternative to a rip cord
28 Coarse type
30 ___ Canal (connector of lakes Ontario and Huron)
33 It intersects the nave
34 Secretary, e.g.
36 Garden no-no, now
37 One of six pieces by Bach
39 Daisy variety
40 Like some questions
42 Vertiginous
44 Wink accompanier
45 "Power Lunch" channel
46 Legendary kicker
47 Legal hearing
50 Sch. in Kingston
51 With 2-Down, seat of Costilla County, Colo.

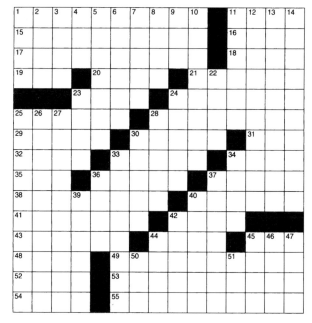

by Brad Wilber

ACROSS

1 Vegetable oil, e.g.
6 College major, briefly
10 Fog
14 Up
15 "Got it"
16 It's often marked with a number
17 Knee problem
19 Very small serving
20 ". . . ___ faith turn to despair": Romeo
21 Capital, usually
23 Leon who won both a Pulitzer and a National Book Award in 1963
24 Smith, e.g.
25 Symbols of freshness
27 Rogers Hornsby's nickname, with "the"
31 Senior ctr.?
33 Garage alternative
34 Before analysis, after "a"
35 Hangers-on
37 Select groups
38 Other drivers (never you, of course)
39 Following group
40 Character lineup
41 It's been put on before
42 Ammunition carrier on wheels
44 Windfall
46 Target of a rabbit punch
49 Like Y, e.g.
52 ___ francese
53 Crown
54 Soft, high-fiber dish
56 Red-bellied trout
57 Topic lead-in
58 Beehive division
59 Firm fear
60 "Saint Joan" playwright
61 Fisherman's basket

DOWN

1 Maker of a historic touchdown
2 Iota
3 Feature of many a big do
4 Neighbor of Monterey Park, briefly
5 Atlas info: Abbr.
6 Filling stations?
7 Had a causerie
8 The sacred bull Apis was his embodiment
9 They're proscribed
10 Jaunty
11 Botanist's angle
12 Fusilli alternative
13 Form of the French "to be"
18 #1 best sellers
22 Apes
26 "Right?"
28 Some clichéd writing
29 Some matériel
30 H.S. subject
31 Do something emotionally to
32 Word preceding various colors
34 Beat
36 They have nagging questions
37 It has valuable questions
39 Game derived from 500 rummy
42 Light carriage with a folding top
43 Even
45 Mexican uncle?
47 Part of the earth's outer layer
48 Oil holder
49 Halite, chemically
50 Be reminiscent of
51 Present occasion, informally
55 Multiple of LXX

by Dana Motley

The New York Times

CROSSWORDS

SMART PUZZLES PRESENTED WITH STYLE

Available at your local bookstore or online at nytimes.com/nytstore.

 St. Martin's Griffin

1

S	A	L	E	M		U	S	E	R		E	M	M	A
O	B	A	M	A		P	A	G	E		R	E	A	L
L	I	T	T	L	E	P	I	G	S		O	N	C	E
E	D	T		A	P	E	D		P	I	T	I	E	S
S	E	E	S	R	E	D		D	I	D	I	N		
		E	K	E		T	I	T	I	C	A	C	A	
A	M	B	L	E		T	R	E	E		T	A	R	
B	I	L	L	Y	G	O	A	T	S	G	R	U	F	F
E	L	I		R	O	C	S		L	O	B	E	S	
D	O	N	T	W	A	L	K		M	I	A			
	D	R	A	T	S		S	A	T	D	O	W	N	
H	O	M	A	G	E		N	A	R	C		M	A	O
A	V	I	D		F	R	E	N	C	H	H	E	N	S
L	A	C	E		U	N	I	T		E	A	G	L	E
F	L	E	D		L	A	N	A		S	T	A	Y	S

2

A	L	A	S		D	A	I	L	Y		J	O	T	S
G	O	R	P		E	R	N	I	E		E	V	E	L
A	L	I	I		C	O	S	T	S		S	E	X	Y
P	L	A	C	E	I	N	T	H	E	S	U	N		
E	S	S	E	X			O	S	U		M	A	T	
			A	B	C	S			N	E	I	G	H	
O	P	S		M	O	R	N	I	N	G	S	T	A	R
C	U	T	E		N	A	I	V	E		E	T	T	E
T	R	A	D	I	N	G	P	O	S	T		S	E	W
A	S	T	A	B		S	R	T	A					
L	E	I		E	O	S			F	L	A	M	E	
	S	I	G	N	O	T	H	E	T	I	M	E	S	
H	A	T	S		T	U	R	O	W		M	U	T	T
Q	T	I	P		A	S	O	N	E		I	S	E	E
S	A	C	S		P	A	P	E	R		T	E	S	S

3

H	E	R	D		P	E	D	A	L		A	C	M	E
M	A	U	I		A	N	N	I	E		F	L	A	X
O	R	G	A	N	T	R	A	N	S	P	L	A	N	T
		Z	E	R	O		T	S	E		S	H	E	
C	H	I		W	O	N	T		E	G	G	S	O	N
A	U	S	T	E	N		W	I	N		M	A	L	T
B	E	A	U	S		F	O	R	E		I	C	E	S
	A	N	T	I	O	X	I	D	A	N	T			
L	A	C	E		N	I	T	S		V	O	I	C	E
I	B	A	R		F	E	W		C	A	R	O	L	S
T	A	S	S	E	L		O	R	A	L		N	I	P
E	L	I		O	A	T		E	N	O	S			
R	O	M	A	N	T	I	C	F	A	N	T	A	S	Y
A	N	O	N		E	M	A	I	L		A	N	T	S
L	E	V	Y		D	E	N	T	S		N	O	E	L

4

Y	O	G	A		A	T	T	I	C		D	O	C	K
E	A	S	T		B	U	R	R	O		O	T	O	E
S	T	A	L	E	B	R	E	A	D		O	T	B	S
			A	R	E	N	A			A	D	A	R	E
E	W	I	N	G		S	T	E	A	L	A	W	A	Y
L	A	O	T	S	E		A	D	I	D	A	S		
A	N	T	I		A	G	A	T	E	S				
L	E	A	S	T	R	E	S	I	S	T	A	N	C	E
			U	N	S	E	N	T		I	C	E	T	
	P	H	O	N	E	S			E	R	R	A	N	T
S	L	A	T	E	R	O	O	F		E	L	A	T	E
N	A	M	E	D			I	R	A	N	I			
I	T	L	L		T	A	L	E	S	O	F	W	O	E
P	E	E	L		S	L	E	E	T		T	I	L	L
E	S	T	O		K	I	D	D	O		S	T	E	M

5

D	U	S	K		P	O	E	M	S		U	S	S	R
A	S	I	A		I	N	D	I	A		S	O	H	O
D	O	G	B	R	E	E	D	E	R		U	F	O	S
E	C	H	O	E	R		A	N	I	M	A	T	E	S
			B	I	R	D			A	L	P			
L	E	A		N	E	U	M	A	N	N		A	C	T
U	N	C	L	E		F	A	T	E		S	L	A	W
N	O	T	E	S	O	F	T	H	E	S	C	A	L	E
A	C	I	D		B	E	T	E		T	I	T	L	E
R	H	O		S	I	L	E	N	C	E		E	S	T
			N	I	T			S	H	A	H			
D	O	D	D	E	R	E	D		E	M	I	N	E	M
A	H	O	Y		S	M	I	L	E	Y	F	A	C	E
M	I	L	L		V	I	N	E	S		I	D	O	L
P	O	L	L		P	R	O	X	Y		S	A	N	D

6

```
A V O N ■ I D L E ■ O R A T E
P A C O ■ T R A M ■ B O X E R
A C C T ■ C A V E ■ S U E D E
C H U R C H W A R D E N ■ ■ ■
H E R E I ■ ■ Y E S D E A R
E L S ■ V I D A ■ E S T A T E
■ ■ D I C I E R ■ R U I N
■ P E R C U S S I O N I S T ■
H I K E ■ ■ H O T T I P ■
B L E A T S ■ P E O N ■ E T H
O L D M A I D ■ ■ E R N I E
■ ■ B I C Y C L E R I D E R
A S S O C ■ I R O N ■ G O R E
M I C A H ■ N E R O ■ E R O S
I S I T I ■ G E E S ■ L A D Y
```

7

```
D O U S E ■ A L F ■ P I Q U E
I D S A Y ■ L E A ■ L A U R A
S I E V E ■ L A W ■ A M I S S
H E R E S J O H N N Y ■ P A Y
■ ■ H O W ■ ■ A M C ■ ■
P A C M A N ■ R E L E A S E D
A C R I D ■ G O L D ■ S U M O
T H E R E S N O I I N T E A M
R E M I ■ M A M A ■ O L D I E
I D E N T I T Y ■ S T E E L S
■ ■ G O T ■ ■ V I A ■ ■
S A M ■ W H E R E S W A L D O
O C E A N ■ Z E N ■ H O A R D
A L I B I ■ R E A ■ I N B A D
P U R S E ■ A L L ■ T E S T S
```

8

```
B E T ■ E F F U S E ■ M A Y S
U Z I ■ F O R A L L ■ A L O E
N R C ■ F L O R I D A K E Y S
T A K E A I M ■ M E D I C O S
■ ■ E N C A M P ■ S O N ■ ■
T A R G E T ■ I N T L ■ J A S
A S T A ■ E D G E ■ P L U N K
S T A G E ■ O P T ■ H I N D I
T O P E R ■ D E S I ■ O K I E
E R E ■ O D O N ■ M I N D E D
■ ■ A D O ■ S I M M E R ■ ■
S I N C E R E ■ S E A L A N T
T H I R D S T R I N G ■ W A R
L O C I ■ A T E A S E ■ E M I
O P E D ■ L A S H E S ■ R E X
```

9

```
W A G S ■ A D D U P ■ E L S E
I D E A ■ L O O S E ■ N O U N
G O L D F I N G E R ■ O W E D
■ ■ D I S S ■ ■ R U S T S
L A M E N T ■ S H R U G ■ ■
E R A S E ■ S T E E L H E A D
T O R T ■ E T E R N E ■ R H O
H U T ■ C L A R E T S ■ R O W
A S H ■ A D L I B S ■ B A R N
L E A D B E L L Y ■ S E N S E
■ ■ V E R S E ■ G O A D E D
A C T O R ■ ■ E L A N ■ ■
R O A R ■ S I L V E R B A C K
A L G A ■ P R E E N ■ A L O E
B A S K ■ Y E A R N ■ G A N G
```

10

```
S T O I C ■ N E A R ■ C O A T
H O N D A ■ U R G E ■ O A T H
E A T I N G C R O W ■ I S E E
A D O ■ C U L ■ G R A N T E E
■ ■ R E N E E ■ I R E ■ ■
■ T A L K I N G T U R K E Y
J O E Y S ■ ■ C O E N ■ A R E
E R T E ■ C A R T S ■ I S I N
E A R ■ T O N Y ■ ■ A M E N S
P L A Y I N G P O S S U M ■
■ ■ A N D ■ T R E S S ■ ■
D E F R A U D ■ G A I ■ B A A
O V E R ■ C R Y I N G W O L F
C A T O ■ T I M E ■ N O R M A
K N E W ■ S P A S ■ S W E A R
```

11

```
A D D S     D O W N     B O B S
D I R T   M A C H O     L A R K
U V E A   A C H E S     O K A Y
L A W R E N C E W E L K
T N T   L I A R     J E E R A T
    H U L A     G O D     A C E
R T E S   C L A M B I S Q U E
A R L E S     O S E     N A U R U
F A I R A M O U N T     H E A P
T I N     L E T       H I L L
S L E E T S     F L E D     W P A
      L I T T L E B O P E E P
M A U I     I R A T E     A L A S
R A Z Z     Z E R O S     A C R E
S H I A     O X E N       R H Y S
```

12

```
L I T U P     M A S T     F A N S
A R O S E     O K R A     O V A L
G E N E R A T I O N     R O S A
E N G     W O N     L E E W A Y
R E A C T O R     H I T S
      A W L     P A N A T E L A
T E T R A     L I V E S A L I E
A T O B     S E X E S     T I E R
M A J O R E D I N     P I A N O
S T O N E A G E     R E O
      A S H E     S E A N C E S
B L O T T O     A P E     O V O
R A V I     R E V E L A T I O N
O R E O     S P I N     S A N K A
W A R N     E A S T     P O S E R
```

13

```
P A T T I     R I F F     A S E A
A V I A N     O M A R     P A T S
J A L F R E D P R U F R O C K
A L L T I M E     G O O P
M O E     T O S S     O N A I R
A N D I E     A W E D     U R I
    P I L S N E R     U L A N
  J J O N A H J A M E S O N
P I E D     L E O T A R D
A M T     B A A S     R A F T S
Z I P P O     F E A R     R I P
    L O F T       S E R R A T E
J D A N F O R T H Q U A Y L E
L A N D     O B O E     S T E E D
O D E S     N I P S     T E D D Y
```

14

```
I C O N     T A P E     B R A N
N A N U     I M A X     A U R A S
S T E M     N I N C O M P O O P
      S O Y     S E R     E M M A
L O C K E     B I R D B R A I N
A M O U R     R E P E A T
P I L L     P O S T A L     D J S
S T E L L A     L E D O U T
E S S     A R E T E S     U N D O
      E L O P E R     S M E A R
D I N G A L I N G     O B E S E
A G O G     E T D     A L B
N O O D L E H E A D     E S P Y
S O N Y S     E R M A     L O G O
    N E E D     T S A R     L U A U
```

15

```
C A C H E     T O S S     C H I C
O C H E R     O B O E     H O O D
S T I N G O P E R A T I O N S
T S A R     S T Y E     E P P S
        I S L E     E W E S
I L K     H O N E Y I M H O M E
D E I C E       X E D     O M E N
T O R A     A M U S E     T A T E
A N O S     M E R       U S H E R
G I V E M E A B U Z Z     A D O
      L I N T     P A I L
    P R O F     P A T H     A L B A
T H E A F R I C A N Q U E E N
W E E D     P E R K     T R I E D
O W L S     I S E E     S A S S Y
```

16

M	I	R	█	R	O	L	A	N	D	█	B	L	A	B
U	N	O	█	E	R	A	S	E	R	█	O	I	L	Y
S	A	G	E	A	D	V	I	C	E	█	Y	E	A	R
K	N	E	L	L	█	A	S	K	A	R	O	U	N	D
S	E	R	B	I	A	█	█	█	M	A	H	█	█	█
█	█	B	A	S	I	L	R	A	T	H	B	O	N	E
A	D	A	█	T	R	E	A	D	█	S	O	C	A	L
D	E	C	O	█	S	A	B	L	E	█	Y	E	N	S
A	L	O	U	D	█	R	I	A	N	T	█	A	A	A
M	I	N	T	C	O	N	D	I	T	I	O	N	█	█
█	█	█	E	L	L	█	█	R	E	D	T	A	G	█
H	Y	B	R	I	D	T	E	A	█	T	O	I	L	E
A	A	R	E	█	H	E	R	B	G	A	R	D	E	N
F	L	E	A	█	A	R	A	B	I	C	█	E	R	E
T	E	A	R	█	T	I	T	A	N	S	█	S	O	S

17

J	O	G	S	█	A	G	A	R	█	O	P	A	R	T
O	R	E	O	█	R	O	L	E	█	B	O	X	E	S
T	E	N	D	E	R	L	O	I	N	S	T	E	A	K
S	M	E	A	R	█	A	T	N	O	█	A	L	P	S
█	█	█	P	R	O	M	O	█	D	O	T	█	█	█
S	O	L	O	█	W	E	N	T	█	L	O	A	T	H
C	H	O	P	I	N	█	O	R	A	L	█	H	A	Y
E	G	G	S	S	U	N	N	Y	S	I	D	E	U	P
N	E	O	█	S	P	E	E	█	S	E	R	A	P	E
T	E	N	S	E	█	A	S	I	A	█	I	D	E	S
█	█	T	I	A	█	P	A	Y	T	V	█	█	█	█
O	A	H	U	█	C	A	L	M	█	L	E	M	M	E
P	E	A	C	H	E	S	A	N	D	C	R	E	A	M
T	R	U	C	E	█	I	T	O	O	█	E	T	N	A
S	O	L	O	N	█	F	E	T	E	█	D	A	N	G

18

A	T	O	Z	█	O	Y	E	Z	█	M	I	S	C	
S	H	O	E	█	M	A	K	E	█	M	A	L	T	A
S	A	N	D	W	E	D	G	E	█	A	V	I	A	N
T	W	A	█	O	L	D	█	C	R	E	A	T	E	
█	M	E	A	T	G	R	I	N	D	E	R	█		
L	O	O	K	A	T	█	E	L	A	N	█			
A	M	A	I	N	█	P	H	O	T	O	C	O	P	Y
R	O	H	E	█	K	R	E	M	E	█	O	R	E	O
S	O	U	V	E	N	I	R	S	█	S	H	I	R	K
█	M	O	M	A	█	T	O	N	G	U	E	█		
A	M	E	R	I	C	A	N	S	U	B	█			
D	E	B	U	N	K	█	E	X	E	█	H	E	M	
L	E	O	N	E	█	S	U	P	E	R	H	E	R	O
I	S	L	A	M	█	A	R	I	D	█	E	L	L	A
B	E	A	T	█	C	I	A	O	█	X	M	E	N	

19

D	U	M	B	█	I	R	I	S	█	Z	O	N	E	D
I	B	E	T	█	N	A	S	A	█	S	M	I	L	E
N	O	N	E	E	D	T	O	T	H	A	N	K	M	E
G	A	L	A	X	Y	█	C	O	Z	I	E	S	T	
S	T	O	M	P	█	J	O	H	N	S	█			
█	█	█	A	L	A	R	M	█	A	S	T	E	R	
G	L	A	D	T	O	B	E	O	F	█	H	O	P	I
N	U	D	I	S	M	█	█	U	S	E	R	I	D	
A	L	E	C	█	A	S	S	I	S	T	A	N	C	E
T	U	N	E	D	█	A	R	O	S	E	█			
█	█	█	R	A	Y	O	N	█	L	A	S	T	S	
T	E	A	S	E	T	S	█	C	L	I	Q	U	E	
I	T	W	A	S	M	Y	P	L	E	A	S	U	R	E
P	A	R	I	S	█	E	V	E	N	█	L	A	N	D
S	L	Y	L	Y	█	S	C	O	T	█	E	B	A	Y

20

J	E	D	█	S	T	A	M	O	S	█	M	O	J	O
A	M	A	█	I	M	P	O	S	E	█	A	W	O	L
B	A	N	A	N	A	B	O	A	T	█	K	N	E	E
B	I	G	T	E	N	█	S	K	A	T	E	█		
E	L	I	A	█	M	E	A	T	W	A	G	O	N	
D	S	T	█	P	E	A	█	O	F	U	S	E		
█	█	R	E	D	R	O	S	E	█	A	N	U	T	
█	T	U	R	N	I	P	T	R	U	C	K	█		
A	R	A	B	█	A	S	T	A	I	R	E			
H	I	R	E	D	█	R	E	N	█	P	G	A		
A	P	P	L	E	C	A	R	T	█	P	I	E	R	
█	B	L	I	G	E	█	D	I	A	N	N	E		
V	E	T	O	█	G	R	A	V	Y	T	R	A	I	N
A	V	O	W	█	A	E	R	I	E	S	█	T	E	A
L	E	N	S	█	R	E	S	E	D	A	█	A	S	S

21

```
S A M I A M █ A L A █ █ T A O
A G E N D A █ W E N T S O L O
P E R S O N A L I T Y Q U I Z
S E E █ █ I F S █ █ P U T T Y
█ █ █ I S L A █ S P E E █ █ █
P R O Q U A R T E R B A C K █
L A P S E █ █ O R O █ L A N A
E N E █ D A R K A G E █ P E T
A U R A █ C O Y █ █ S H R E W
█ P A T C H W O R K Q U I L T
█ █ O L E S █ S A S H █ █ █
M T I D A █ O V I █ █ E E E
M I N D Y O U R P S A N D Q S
E M I S S A R Y █ E V E N U P
S E T █ █ K I X █ R E T A I N
```

22

```
S E Z █ U T T E R █ R A N D B
I L E █ N O O S E █ A D O R E
T I R E S O M E W I N D B A G
A H O L E █ █ I N S █ I T S █
T U S K E D W A R T H O G █ █
█ █ █ S N O O Z E █ O L D I E
J A M █ L E O █ P R I E S T █
P R O M P T S █ P E T N A M E
E M B E R S █ R E T █ █ L E S
G E S S O █ H E A R S T █ █ █
█ C A P E A F R I K A N E R █
E R E █ O T T █ █ E L E N A █
D A N I S H P H Y S I C I S T
G R E T A █ I M E A N █ G U T
E A S E L █ N O N O S █ H E Y
```

23

```
F U M E █ S E M I █ B A S I N
U N I V █ A X E D █ A C H O O
S I D E █ L I M E █ S T E W S
S T A N D A T E A S E █ D A Y
Y E S S I R █ █ S A M B A █ █
█ █ O B I E S █ P A R T E D █
I C U █ S E V E N █ N E E D Y
L A P D █ D A T E S █ W A G E
S M A R T █ C O A L S █ R E D
A E N E A S █ F R I T O █ █ █
█ D I X O N █ █ M O P T O P █
B A A █ F L O R I D A T E C H
A S T R O █ W A C O █ S R T A
S T E E R █ A N E W █ I R E S
H I M O M █ Y A R N █ N A T E
```

24

```
S T A G E █ T A N G O █ H I T
A R I E S █ I C E A X █ U F O
C U R T A I N C A L L █ M O P
█ █ █ B U S H █ █ I N A R T
B A B Y █ B A T H S P O N G E
U N O █ A N T E U P █ D C O N
G O B A D █ █ A N A █ S O T S
█ █ B L O O D S T R E A M █ █
J A Y E █ M I I █ █ S T E R N
I L K A █ N O N F A T █ D A B
G U N S L I N G E R █ S Y N C
S M I T E █ █ I M A C █ █ █
A N G █ T H I N G S D R A W N
W A H █ B A C O N █ Z A I R E
S E T █ E D I T S █ E M M Y S
```

25

```
A C M E █ R A N O N █ F U R Y
B I A S █ I R A T E █ O N E A
C O C A █ P A N I C █ C A P P
█ H U M P B A C K W A I L █
A V E █ A L I █ █ O L D E R
B A T T L E C R E A K █ E T E
A L E U T █ █ E R G █ I D E A
█ █ F A R M G R O A N █ █
S E C T █ A A A █ R C P T S
O A R █ B E L L A N D H O W L
P R O S Y █ █ T O E █ B O Y
█ M A K E S A B O O B O O █
H A T E █ E L A N D █ A X L E
E R I E █ R U R A L █ H E E L
S K A T █ A M B L E █ U S A F
```

26

```
L O F T   E B O L A   O M S K
I D I O   N O R A D   M U N I
F I V E S T A R G E N E R A L
T E E T E R       A L A I N
    C O E   F I V E B E L L S
S T E T S   A F I R S T
H A N O I   T S A R   G A D
E X T E N T       S I C I L Y
D I S   G U L F   N O M D E
    T A I P E I   P U M A S
T A K E S F I V E   O N E
O D E T S       A R T F U L
Q U A R T E R P A S T F I V E
U L N A   R A B B I   O V E N
E T E S   A T S E A   R E A D
```

27

```
S W A M   B O O M   S A B L E
O H I O   I S L E   T U T U S
D I D O   S L A T   E D E N S
  M A N W H O F E L L I N T O
    S H O     I L O
D S C   O P S   B L A T A N T
U P H O L S T E R Y   A M I R
N A I V E   E T A   S P I N E
E S N E   M A C H I N E N O W
S M A R T E D   E G O   O S S
    S R I     I R E
F U L L Y R E C O V E R E D
A L O E S   W O K E   E L A N
I N S E T   E C R U   C L I O
R A S P S   S O A P   T A S S
```

28

```
S P A T   M I K A D O   A G R
U R N S   G U N N E R   R O E
B O O K E M D A N N O   M E G
P R I E S T   V I A   S O S A
L A N D S   N E E D A L I F T
O T T   O V A   A R A R A T
T E S T   W I N G   O P E R A
    I T S F O R Y O U
S A U D I   S W E E   P I C A
E L N I N O   E N D   N O M
L I K E A R O C K   E L T O N
F E N D   S R O   O L E O L E
I N O   P I C K U P L I N E S
S E W   I N H E R E   L E S T
H E N   T O S S I N   A R T Y
```

29

```
T I L T   A B O V E   F I J I
O D O R   B O R A X   L O O N
M A G I   A R E N T   O W E N
  S O N E S N O S E   W A Y S
    K L E E     N Y E
S C R E E D   U N D E R M Y
O R A T E   G R E E N   I A N
R U N S   N A I A D   A L L A
E S C   P E N A L   M U L T I
  T H R O U G H   R E D E A L
    H E R   Z I T I
Q U A Y   O P P O S A B L E
T R I M   S A O N E   L A T S
I D L E   I N N E R   E C R U
P U S S   S E E D S   S E E P
```

30

```
B A L E   S P E A R   S C R A P
A L A N   A I S L E   T R A S H
S O R T   F E T A L   A O R T A
I F V E G E T A R I A N S E A T
S T A R E     M E L D S
    O S L O   D L I   M O O
E V E L   W A I L   O S W A L D
V E G E T A B L E S W H A T D O
I S A I A H   S A K E   D E E R
L T D   L I P   F I D O
    M E L O N     W A L E S
H U M A N I T A R I A N S E A T
E V E N T   A B O M B   P A G E
L E A S E   T O T A L   I S L E
P A L E D   O B E S E   C H E R
```

31

C	R	A	G		U	B	O	L	T		F	A	Z	E
R	U	L	E		S	A	T	I	E		E	X	E	C
A	M	E	N		A	L	I	N	E		L	E	N	O
B	O	X	O	F	F	I	C	E	H	I	T			
B	R	I	A	R			A	E	R	I	A	L	S	
E	S	S		A	R	M	W	R	E	S	T	L	E	R
			F	I	O	N	A			C	O	M	O	
	H	O	L	D	O	N	T	I	G	H	T			
A	J	A	R			D	E	R	R	Y				
S	U	I	T	S	T	O	A	T	E	E		S	E	C
S	T	R	I	K	E	R			A	P	P	L	Y	
		F	I	N	I	S	H	S	T	R	O	N	G	
F	I	J	I		N	O	H	I	T		A	K	I	N
O	K	I	E		I	L	I	K	E		N	E	N	E
B	E	G	S		S	E	V	E	R		K	N	O	T

32

B	A	H		F	A	L	L		C	A	T	N	I	P
O	R	U		A	S	E	A		A	I	R	A	C	E
A	I	M		C	H	I	C	K	F	L	I	C	K	S
R	A	B	B	I		S	E	N	T		F	R	E	T
	L	E	A	S			E	A	R	L	E	S	S	
J	O	E	Y	L	A	W	R	E	N	C	E			
A	M	P		S	A	H	I	B		A	R	N	A	Z
M	A	I	M		B	I	G	O	T		S	E	R	B
S	N	E	R	D		S	O	N	I	C		R	N	A
			C	O	L	T	R	E	V	O	L	V	E	R
A	L	C	O	H	O	L			O	M	O	O		
L	I	E	F		Q	E	I	I		E	X	U	R	B
C	A	L	F	M	U	S	C	L	E	S		S	O	O
O	R	T	E	G	A		K	I	R	I		L	A	C
A	S	S	E	R	T		Y	A	R	N		Y	M	A

33

O	L	I	V	E	R		O	K	L	A	H	O	M	A
M	I	N	O	S	O		S	P	A	M	A	L	O	T
A	V	A	L	O	N		L	A	V	A	L	I	E	R
R	E	N	T		C	O	X	E	S		N	S	A	
R	U	E		T	R	A		D	S	C				
	P	R	O	V	E	R	B	S			H	A	I	R
		C	A	B	A	R	E	T		A	N	N	E	
E	C	R	U		E	V	I	T	A		L	Y	N	X
P	H	I	L		C	A	N	D	I	D	E			
A	I	D	A		N	E	O	N	A	T	A	L		
	R	S	A		W	T	S		N	A	T			
D	E	N		C	L	O	W	N		F	A	M	E	
O	V	E	R	R	I	D	E		J	O	R	D	A	N
C	A	R	O	U	S	E	L		F	R	I	E	Z	E
S	H	O	W	B	O	A	T		K	I	S	M	E	T

34

S	C	A	L	P		A	M	A	S	S		T	D	S
O	M	N	I	A		L	A	C	T	O		H	O	T
F	O	U	R	T	E	E	N	R	E	D		E	R	Y
A	N	T	I	T	A	X		E	N	A	B	L	E	R
			I	C	E	S				A	M	M	O	
O	L	A	F		H	I	T	M	E	A	G	A	I	N
R	O	S	I	E		A	I	D	S					
D	O	U	B	L	E	O	R	N	O	T	H	I	N	G
			L	E	N	D			A	U	D	I	O	
I	L	L	T	A	K	E	O	N	E		M	O	T	O
M	E	A	N			M	E	T	A					
P	A	T	T	E	R	S		S	C	R	A	P	E	R
E	S	E		R	O	L	L	T	H	E	D	I	C	E
D	E	N		A	D	U	E	L		N	I	E	C	E
E	S	T		S	E	E	M	E		A	N	S	E	L

35

C	L	A	M	P		A	R	M	O	R		I	S	H
R	A	D	I	I		L	E	A	V	E		C	P	A
E	Z	O	N	T	H	E	E	Y	E	S		S	I	N
M	A	R	I	S	A		F	O	R	E	S	T	E	D
E	R	N	O		H	M	S		K	N	U	R	L	S
			N	C	A	A		T	I	T	L	E		
B	A	S	S	O		I	D	O	L		K	E	E	N
U	S	A		Q	P	D	O	L	L	S		T	O	E
S	P	C	A		R	E	E	L		T	A	S	S	O
		O	L	D	E	N		E	D	E	N			
F	U	N	G	U	S		A	D	O		A	L	S	O
L	I	T	A	N	I	E	S		E	R	R	A	T	A
E	N	E		C	D	C	H	A	R	A	C	T	E	R
S	T	S		A	I	R	E	D		T	H	I	N	E
H	A	T		N	O	U	N	S		S	Y	N	O	D

36

```
T O R M E   D I C E   C L U B
O P I U M   I M A X   R O S E
M I S S I L E U N I V E R S E
S E E K   O D S   T A V E R N
      O O O   A F T A
  T E X T I L E M E S S A G E
R I D   T E E N I E   S O U P
O B E Y S   S A N   E E R I E
T I N A   A L M O N D   T O E
C A S T I L E I R O N P A N
    I N K Y   V A R
C O N T R A   I O U   O S S O
H O S T I L E C O M P U T E R
O N E L   I H O P   A S Y E T
P A C E   S S N S   S T E P S
```

37

```
L I M E   L A M B   R I O T S
A S E C   A L O E   E R R O R
T A L C   T E R R A F I R M A
H A B E A S C O R P U S
E C A S H   N A B S   C P A
    I A M S   S A S H E S
J O N G   B U L B   L I E N S
A R O N   A B O V O   N E N E
P A D U A   J U D O   E R S T
A T O M I C   S H A Q
N E Z   M U S H   R U S T S
    A L E A I A C T A E S T
S E M P E R I D E M   N E A R
E P E E S   N E R O   O T R A
W A R D S   T R O N   N O S Y
```

38

```
W A S P S   W K R P   M S R P
A G O R A   O L I O   O T O E
X A X E S   L U G S   O P A L
    * S O F T H E T R A D E
I M A M   P E E T   R E * S
Q U E E N E D   S U E D
T U R N E D   * I S E   J I F
E M O T E   S O D A   P I N E
S U B S   R A R E   V E N T I
T U E   H A T *   H O A X E S
    K I W I   T E N C E N T
  D C I V   R O A M   E D D Y
J E A N E K I R K P A *
A I R S   A C T E   N I E C E
N O D E   O A H U   D E L L A
E N * Y   S L O P   A S S E T
```

Squares marked with a * read TRICK in one direction and TREAT in the other. Three have TRICK across and TREAT down; the others have the reverse.

39

```
C H A L K S   E P E E   C A T
L A D I E S   U R N S   A L E
A S I A N S   L O V E L I F E
S T E I N   R E N O   E R I N
H O U S E P A R T Y   G O E S
    E L E V   O S H A
S T L   N E E   U T I C A
T W O K I N D S O F B O A T S
S I X A M   P L O   N R A
    N A P S   A C E S
B O O S   I C E F I S H I N G
L P G A   P H I S   C U T I E
A I R S P E E D   M O T I V E
N N E   A T M E   I R I S E S
D E S   Y S E R   A T N I N E
```

40

```
B O U L D E R     B A R R E D
O N S E C O N D   A P I E C E
L E G A L E S E   R E V S U P
D I R K     S O D S   T A R
E R A   B A S E D   B O D E
R O N   A L E X E I   O R O S
  N T E S T S     S E W E R S
      I T E S   B A L E
B O R D E R     A B I D E S
O B O E   S O V I E T   N I S
A S T R   V I L L E   T N T
R C A   B E A T     B E A R
D U T I E S   A L A C A R T E
E R O D E S   L A B O R E R S
R E R A T E     P O S E D A S
```

41

```
N E W M A N ■ O N T H E W A Y
E X H U M E ■ P I R A N H A S
W H E R E T H E B O Y S A R E
S I N I S T E R ■ N E U T E R
■ L I A ■ V E A L ■ S R I ■
N A F T A ■ P T A S ■ E N D O
I R A I S E ■ E N O S ■ T E X
S A L C H O W ■ E L E V A T E
A T L ■ E N I D ■ D E L R A Y
N E I L ■ S P E C ■ D A N C E
■ N I A ■ E E R O ■ D A H ■
A R L E N E ■ P E R M I T M E
W H O N E E D S E N E M I E S
L I V E A L I E ■ O N I O N S
S N E E R S A T ■ T U R N T O
```

42

```
S C O T S ■ I M A C S ■ A S H
C O U R T ■ M A R I S ■ N E A
U N T I E D F R O N T ■ T A J
B A B B L E ■ C D E ■ S O L I
A N Y ■ L A S H ■ P A I N ■
■ M A R T I A L B L I S S
D A T A ■ E N D E A V O R S
I N H U M A N ■ E X T E N T S
A N A L O G O U S ■ R I A S
L A N D I N G S T I E S
■ K I L O ■ H E L D ■ R I M
G W Y N ■ S U E ■ U B O A T S
L A O ■ I T S R E V E R S E D
I C U ■ V I D E O ■ R E T R O
B O S ■ S C A D S ■ G L A S S
```

43

```
A M S ■ S W A M I ■ B O O Z E
C A P I T A L O F F E N S E S
T H E D E F E N S E R E S T S
O R L E ■ A T E ■ A A A
R E L A P S ■ A Y E A R ■
■ A U L D ■ E L S A
A D M I S S I O N T O B A I L
C O U R T A P P E A R A N C E
M O T I O N S T O S T R I K E
E R E S ■ E S S E ■
■ H I R E D ■ E A S T L A
A L G ■ V I M ■ T I O S
J U R Y O F O N E S P E E R S
E X P E R T T E S T I M O N Y
T E S T Y ■ E S Q U E ■ N E R
```

44

```
A S E C ■ B O F F O ■ S H U E
[THE]L M A ■ S M[OLD]E R ■ H E R[MAN]
N A I R ■ I N E R T ■ R I G A
S P L E N D I D ■ B I N E T
■ F E E S ■ C H I N E S E
A Z O R E S ■ F L A S K ■
H O W E ■ C L A R O ■ S S W
E R N E S T H E M I N G W A Y
M A S ■ T I E U P ■ I A M S
■ S I T A R ■ C H U T E S
E G O T R I P ■ B A I L ■
R I L E S ■ E G G T I M E R
R V E R ■ R E S I N ■ A C M E
[AND]E A N ■ E A[THE]R E ■ N A U[SEA]
S S N S ■ C U R L Y ■ I N S T
```

45

```
D O T E D U ■ S M E E ■ D O M
A V O W A L ■ H I L L ■ E N O
P A R E N T H E S E S ■ N E V
■ R A R E ■ S E E P A G E
P A T ■ A L P O ■ O L I O
I M A M S ■ P O U N D S I G N
P E L O T A ■ T R O U T ■
E X C L A M A T I O N M A R K
■ I R A N I ■ K E E P O N
A M P E R S A N D ■ S N I P E
S O U R ■ T G I F ■ A Y E
S C R E E C H ■ S E A S ■
I K E ■ T H E S H I F T K E Y
S E E ■ N E M O ■ G R E E N E
I D S ■ A W A Y ■ N O M A D S
```

46

P	A	N	G	■	A	B	O	M	B	S	■	S	E	A
A	M	O	R	■	R	E	B	A	L	E	■	A	X	L
Y	U	R	I	G	A	G	A	R	I	N	■	T	I	E
E	S	T	E	E	M	■	M	I	N	D	S	E	T	S
R	E	E	V	E	■	S	A	N	I	B	E	L	■	■
■	■	E	R	S	T	■	■	A	L	L	A	H	■	■
B	A	S	S	■	A	R	E	S	■	C	L	I	V	E
A	M	P	■	S	P	U	T	N	I	K	■	T	O	W
R	O	A	S	T	■	T	A	O	S	■	S	E	W	N
D	I	C	T	A	■	■	R	H	E	E	■	■	■	■
■	■	E	A	R	H	A	R	T	■	L	A	S	S	O
F	E	R	N	D	A	L	E	■	S	I	L	T	E	D
E	R	A	■	A	L	A	N	S	H	E	P	A	R	D
T	I	C	■	T	E	N	D	T	O	■	U	R	G	E
A	C	E	■	E	N	D	S	U	P	■	P	E	E	R

47

G	A	B	O	R	■	C	H	I	P	■	A	R	A	B
A	G	R	E	E	■	O	A	T	H	■	M	E	G	R
G	E	O	R	G	E	C	L	O	O	■	O	N	L	Y
A	D	A	■	A	S	O	F	■	N	E	S	T	E	A
■	■	D	E	L	T	A	■	M	E	W	■	S	T	N
G	R	A	C	I	E	■	L	A	Y	E	R	■	■	■
R	E	X	H	A	R	R	I	S	■	■	R	E	H	A	B
A	V	E	O	■	S	A	M	O	A	■	T	E	L	E
Y	E	S	E	S	■	B	E	N	S	T	I	L	L	E
■	■	S	A	P	I	D	■	S	I	M	P	E	R	■
O	V	A	■	G	A	D	■	K	I	T	E	D	■	■
R	E	G	I	O	N	■	P	I	S	A	■	E	S	P
B	R	A	N	■	F	A	L	L	I	N	G	S	T	A
E	N	I	D	■	R	A	U	L	■	I	N	K	E	R
D	E	N	Y	■	Y	A	M	S	■	C	U	S	P	S

48

F	R	A	U	■	B	A	K	E	D	■	C	O	L	E
R	E	V	S	■	O	X	I	D	E	■	A	V	I	V
E	G	O	S	■	R	E	T	I	E	■	F	A	Z	E
N	A	W	■	I	N	S	E	C	R	E	T	■	■	■
C	L	E	A	N	■	■	T	E	N	A	B	L	E	■
H	E	R	C	U	L	E	S	■	O	N	I	O	N	■
■	■	E	R	O	S	I	V	E	■	O	N	T	■	■
■	S	I	D	E	S	P	L	I	T	T	I	N	G	■
U	P	S	■	E	N	A	C	T	E	D	■	■	■	■
R	I	N	G	S	■	S	E	A	L	E	D	U	P	■
I	N	T	E	N	S	E	■	L	A	Y	T	O	■	■
■	■	T	O	P	S	T	O	R	Y	■	N	E	T	■
M	E	A	L	■	I	T	A	K	E	■	S	A	R	A
R	E	D	O	■	F	E	T	I	D	■	S	M	U	T
S	L	A	W	■	F	R	I	E	S	■	S	O	S	O

49

■	L	I	L	A	C	S	■	T	I	E	■	P	A	K
D	E	V	I	L	L	E	■	I	N	A	■	I	C	E
I	T	A	L	I	A	N	■	A	T	R	O	P	H	Y
C	N	N	■	Q	U	A	D	■	A	L	B	E	E	S
T	O	T	R	U	S	T	I	S	G	O	O	D	■	■
■	■	H	O	E	■	G	I	L	B	E	R	T	S	■
C	A	P	E	T	■	D	I	X	I	E	■	E	A	U
H	I	R	E	■	N	O	T	T	O	■	D	A	R	N
A	D	A	■	J	O	N	A	H	■	P	U	M	P	S
R	A	T	I	O	N	A	L	■	O	R	E	■	■	■
■	■	T	R	U	S	T	I	S	B	E	T	T	E	R
A	S	L	A	N	T	■	S	E	E	S	■	H	R	E
S	T	E	N	C	I	L	■	P	R	O	V	E	R	B
T	O	O	■	E	C	O	■	T	O	R	E	R	O	S
O	W	N	■	S	K	Y	■	A	N	T	L	E	R	■

50

A	V	O	W	■	A	M	E	N	D	■	G	A	W	K
V	I	D	I	■	L	E	R	O	I	■	A	G	E	E
E	V	E	L	■	T	S	A	R	S	■	P	U	N	Y
R	O	A	D	T	E	S	T	■	G	R	E	A	T	S
■	■	I	M	R	E	■	D	U	O	■	■	■	■	■
E	V	A	D	E	■	D	A	Y	I	N	■	V	I	M
L	I	N	E	N	S	■	P	A	S	A	D	E	N	A
U	S	D	A	■	M	A	L	D	E	■	A	R	T	I
D	O	N	S	H	U	L	A	■	S	E	R	V	E	D
E	R	O	■	A	R	E	N	A	■	A	K	E	R	S
■	■	■	K	F	C	■	M	A	S	H	■	■	■	■
A	P	O	G	E	E	■	R	U	P	T	U	R	E	D
C	O	O	L	■	T	H	E	S	E	■	M	A	Z	E
M	O	P	E	■	T	U	N	E	R	■	O	K	R	A
E	L	S	E	■	E	N	T	R	Y	■	R	E	A	L

51

S	P	A	R	■	I	N	F	O	■	M	I	C	A
C	A	N	I	■	P	O	E	M	■	M	C	C	O	Y
A	R	G	O	■	A	M	I	E	■	O	N	I	O	N
P	I	S	T	O	N	E	N	G	I	N	E	■		
E	S	T	A	T	E	■	A	R	R	I	V	A	L
■	■	C	O	M	E	S	■	O	O	L	A	L	A
B	R	E	T	E	A	S	T	O	N	E	L	L	I	S
Y	E	A	■	P	E	N	■	L	E	I
F	I	R	S	T	O	N	E	T	O	B	L	I	N	K
A	N	N	E	A	L	■	P	O	L	I	O
R	E	S	E	L	L	S	■	D	A	W	N	E	D
■	H	E	A	R	T	O	F	S	T	O	N	E
R	A	V	E	N	■	T	O	D	O	■	I	T	A	L
E	X	E	R	T	■	A	F	I	G	■	D	I	C	E
P	E	T	E	■	S	U	E	Y	■	E	N	T	S

52

C	B	S	■	C	O	L	T	■	U	T	A	H	A	N
O	R	A	T	O	R	I	O	■	N	O	S	A	L	E
A	U	T	O	M	A	T	E	■	C	O	S	S	E	T
S	N	A	P	P	L	E	■	C	O	L	I	N	■	
T	O	N	G	A	■	B	O	N	■	S	O	L	E
■	U	N	I	V	E	R	S	I	T	I	E	S
R	A	I	N	Y	S	E	A	S	O	N	■	D	A	S
E	D	S	■	M	A	R	S	A	L	A	■	E	R	A
T	I	O	■	E	A	S	T	G	E	R	M	A	N	Y
R	E	C	O	N	C	I	L	E	D	T	O	■		
Y	U	R	I	■	H	O	Y	■	I	D	E	S	T
■	A	L	B	A	N	■	C	A	S	E	L	A	W
A	R	T	E	R	Y	■	D	O	C	T	R	I	N	E
C	H	E	R	I	E	■	N	O	M	I	N	A	T	E
T	O	S	S	E	S	■	A	L	E	C	■	S	A	D

53

A	C	T	F	O	R	■	P	R	I	C	E	T	A	G
M	A	H	A	L	O	■	R	I	G	H	T	A	R	M
O	P	E	N	E	R	■	E	C	L	E	C	T	I	C
R	I	C	■	G	Y	M	S	H	O	E	S	■		
A	T	R	A	■	A	U	T	O	S	■	S	H	H
L	A	U	G	H	A	T	M	E	■	E	A	P	O	E
■	S	O	U	T	H	E	R	N	C	R	O	S	S
C	H	A	R	G	E	■	D	A	N	T	E	S
M	A	D	A	M	E	S	P	E	A	K	E	R	■	
D	I	E	S	E	■	P	I	C	K	E	T	E	R	S
R	R	S	■	T	O	U	G	H	■	T	M	E	N
■	D	I	R	T	P	O	O	R	■	O	D	A
A	B	R	O	G	A	T	E	■	D	O	O	V	E	R
H	E	I	G	H	T	E	N	■	D	O	T	E	L	L
S	T	P	E	T	E	R	S	■	S	T	O	R	M	Y

54

S	T	O	P	S	I	N	■	Q	U	I	V	I	V	E
H	O	P	I	N	T	O	■	U	N	M	O	R	A	L
I	R	E	P	E	A	T	■	A	C	U	T	E	L	Y
A	N	N	E	E	■	A	F	R	■	S	E	L	E	S
T	O	S	S	■	B	R	U	T	E	■	D	A	R	E
S	U	E	■	F	R	I	Z	Z	L	E	■	N	I	E
U	T	A	H	J	A	Z	Z	■	E	L	U	D	E	S
■	■	M	O	N	E	Y	B	A	G	S	■			
R	E	C	O	R	D	■	M	E	N	I	S	C	U	S
E	P	A	■	D	E	C	A	G	O	N	■	R	K	O
N	I	L	E	■	D	O	T	E	R	■	B	A	R	N
E	T	O	N	S	■	A	H	N	■	C	O	N	A	N
G	O	R	E	T	E	X	■	T	W	I	N	K	I	E
E	M	I	R	A	T	E	■	L	A	R	G	E	N	T
D	E	C	O	Y	E	D	■	E	N	C	O	D	E	S

55

G	O	F	O	R	A	D	I	P	■	S	O	P	O	R
A	B	O	R	I	G	I	N	E	■	C	L	A	R	O
V	E	R	K	L	E	M	P	T	■	A	S	S	A	Y
A	R	T	I	E	■	M	R	T	■	L	O	T	T	A
G	O	W	N	■	Q	E	I	I	■	E	N	R	O	L
E	N	O	■	T	U	R	N	E	R	■	A	R	I
■	■	A	H	A	■	T	S	U	N	A	M	I	S
A	M	B	I	E	N	T	■	T	S	E	L	I	O	T
Q	U	I	X	O	T	I	C	■	H	A	L	■		
U	S	A	■	A	M	U	L	E	T	■	R	A	J
A	S	S	A	D	■	E	R	A	S	■	M	E	T	O
T	E	T	R	A	■	L	A	O	■	G	A	T	O	S
I	D	I	O	T	■	A	C	T	S	A	L	O	N	E
C	U	R	S	E	■	G	A	Z	A	S	T	R	I	P
S	P	E	E	D	■	S	O	U	L	P	A	T	C	H

56

ASBADASBADCANBE
THEREYOUGOAGAIN
LITTLEORNOTHING
■MAST■TRIM■AVGS
■■■CYS■■■ISEE■
FAJITA■■PIC■■
OVERANDDONEWITH
AIRAMERICARADIO
MAKEARESOLUTION
■■LSD■■INTONE
■PLIE■■EKE■■
BAIN■KANE■JOAD
LIBERALDEMOCRAT
ANYPORTINASTORM
SEATTLESEAHAWKS

57

LEAVESABADTASTE
ARTAPPRECIATION
BYTRIALANDERROR
■■AMC■OMEN■ORTO
LEGIST■■TUPELO
AGIN■EKES■SHEET
TORT■TINAFEY■■
ESL■FONDLED■ALA
■■GONDOLA■IRIS
FRERE■AWES■MMES
RAREST■■TOEOUT
IMIN■RICE■MAR■
ESCAPEMECHANISM
DEADASADOORNAIL
ASSESSMENTROLLS

58

DENSEFOG■APLOMB
EXITLANE■PREMIE
BENEDICT■TENANT
SCORELESS■STRUT
■■■OSS■CELS■STE
SPLIT■SADIE■HER
LEAD■SPRATS■AMI
EATS■HARTE■BRAD
ESE■DORIES■EIRE
PHI■EARED■KAFKA
TEN■CLOD■MAS■■
ILLER■WATERPIPE
GLIDER■WARZONES
HEFNER■APIARIES
TREADS■YATITTLE

59

INASPOT■■CANTBE
CARALARM■RCCOLA
IBEFOREE■ICARUS
CONEY■EDAM■ANET
LBAR■XFILES■IRE
ESS■SCOUTSHONOR
■■STORM■COSTAS
■POIROT■LETSON■
SIFTER■SANAA■■
ONTHEDOCKET■PIS
DET■PIXIES■SANE
ACID■NOPE■SKIDS
POMONA■IRSAUDIT
ONESET■OILGAUGE
PESTLE■■EYESPOT

60

SQUEEGEES■OHWOW
AUSTRALIA■DUANE
NONEATALL■INITS
ETAS■EYES■EATIT
REV■■SNEAD■NAPE
■DYER■ENDUP■STR
■■■NOS■SIMOLEON
BIGTALK■PALACES
OVERDONE■SOS■■
RET■SPAMS■STIR
AHAT■SPOTS■NOB
BALES■STEP■ABBY
ODIST■AIRINGOUT
RIFLE■CONCOURSE
ATEAM■KNEEPANTS

61

M	Y	S	P	A	C	E	■	■	G	O	S	S	I	P
I	O	M	O	T	H	S	■	R	E	D	W	I	N	E
S	K	I	P	O	U	T	■	O	N	E	F	L	A	T
S	O	T	■	P	G	A	T	O	U	R	■	E	P	I
T	O	T	O	■	S	T	A	T	S	■	S	N	I	T
E	N	E	M	Y	■	E	R	E	■	T	I	T	L	E
P	O	N	I	E	S	■	T	R	O	U	N	C	E	S
■	■	G	A	L	L	■	S	A	N	A	■	■	■	■
I	M	N	O	T	Y	O	U	■	T	I	T	H	E	S
D	R	E	S	S	■	V	C	R	■	C	R	E	P	T
E	S	T	H	■	B	E	L	O	W	■	A	R	I	D
A	L	F	■	H	A	S	A	C	O	W	■	E	T	E
M	A	L	A	I	S	E	■	K	R	A	T	I	O	N
E	T	I	C	K	E	T	■	O	R	I	G	A	M	I
N	E	X	T	E	L	■	■	N	Y	T	I	M	E	S

62

F	A	T	S	W	A	L	L	E	R	■	W	E	B	S
I	G	E	T	A	R	O	U	N	D	■	A	Q	U	A
R	E	N	O	N	E	V	A	D	A	■	L	U	S	T
E	L	O	P	E	■	E	N	L	S	■	L	I	L	I
F	I	N	S	■	B	I	D	E	■	■	F	A	R	
O	N	E	■	D	Y	N	A	S	T	■	J	A	N	E
X	E	R	O	X	E	S	■	S	I	L	E	X	E	S
■	■	■	W	I	N	■	■	L	O	S	■	■	■	■
Z	I	L	L	I	O	N	■	A	T	A	T	I	M	E
H	M	O	S	■	W	E	E	D	E	D	■	N	O	N
I	E	S	■	■	P	R	O	D	■	L	U	N	G	
V	A	T	S	■	S	T	E	P	■	S	I	T	K	A
A	N	A	T	■	A	U	C	T	I	O	N	E	E	R
G	I	R	L	■	I	N	T	E	R	F	E	R	E	D
O	T	T	O	■	D	E	S	E	R	T	R	O	S	E

63

■	Y	O	U	O	K	■	S	T	E	M	L	E	S	S
B	E	R	N	I	E	■	C	O	R	S	E	L	E	T
L	A	D	I	D	A	■	U	N	I	Q	U	E	L	Y
A	H	E	M	■	A	D	I	E	U	■	M	A	X	
S	I	R	P	A	U	L	■	S	A	W	■	■	■	■
E	M	B	R	I	T	T	L	E	■	D	R	U	S	E
■	F	L	E	S	H	I	E	S	T	■	O	N	E	A
B	I	A	S	■	E	M	O	T	E	■	N	L	A	T
I	N	N	S	■	R	A	N	R	A	G	G	E	D	■
P	E	K	E	S	■	S	E	A	S	O	N	T	W	O
■	■	■	D	T	S	■	D	E	P	U	T	E	S	
P	O	I	■	P	O	D	I	A	■	M	A	L	T	
S	A	N	T	E	R	I	A	■	P	O	B	B	L	E
S	T	R	A	T	T	O	N	■	D	U	E	L	E	R
T	H	E	B	E	A	R	S	■	F	I	R	E	R	■

64

T	H	E	T	H	I	N	G	I	S	■	E	N	O	W
S	O	C	I	A	L	C	A	L	L	■	L	O	R	I
A	N	O	T	H	E	R	D	A	Y	■	I	W	O	N
R	E	L	O	A	N	■	■	E	L	A	Y	N	E	
■	■	■	S	E	W	E	R	■	A	H	O	O	T	
C	A	S	E	■	S	E	R	U	M	S	■	U	M	A
E	L	M	S	T	■	B	A	B	U	S	H	K	A	S
A	L	A	M	O	D	E	■	I	M	E	A	N	I	T
S	A	L	E	M	S	L	O	T	■	S	T	O	N	E
E	N	L	■	C	L	O	R	I	S	■	E	W	E	R
F	A	T	H	A	■	S	E	N	O	R	■	■	■	■
I	D	I	O	T	S	■	■	R	E	G	A	L	E	
R	A	M	S	■	U	T	N	E	R	E	A	D	E	R
E	L	E	E	■	R	A	G	G	E	D	Y	A	N	N
S	E	R	A	■	G	O	O	G	L	Y	E	Y	E	S

65

P	L	A	N	B	■	T	O	T	S	■	C	C	U	P
E	O	L	I	A	N	H	A	R	P	■	O	R	N	E
P	O	I	N	D	E	X	T	E	R	■	T	E	D	S
E	N	T	E	R	S	■	H	O	U	S	E	P	E	T
■	■	■	R	A	C	E	S	■	C	A	D	E	T	
R	A	M	■	P	A	X	■	S	E	R	A	P	E	S
A	V	I	S	■	F	I	J	I	■	O	Z	A	R	K
J	A	C	Q	U	E	L	I	N	E	D	U	P	R	E
A	S	K	U	P	■	E	M	I	R	■	R	E	E	D
S	T	E	A	D	E	D	■	S	A	S	■	R	D	S
■	M	Y	R	O	N	■	H	E	S	H	E	■	■	■
S	A	F	E	S	I	D	E	■	M	A	L	O	N	E
A	T	I	C	■	G	A	S	G	U	Z	Z	L	E	R
R	E	N	U	■	M	I	S	S	S	A	I	G	O	N
G	Y	N	T	■	A	S	E	A	■	M	E	A	N	S

66

ENTEBBE · WHATAMI
SIERRAS · NOWISER
TENNESSEEWALKER
ACTIVEINTERESTS
RESEEDED
ZANINESS
SPANISHOMELETTE
EUROPEANTHEATER
CREASERESISTANT
OLDHANDS
EARHOLES
REALESTATEAGENT
ISEAGERTOPLEASE
SAOTOME · MOVESUP
KINESIS · STASHES

67

CLEW · HEATDAMAGE
LASH · ERRORRATES
ESPY · FRONTAXLES
OER · ETON · BANA
PRETZEL · CARAWAY
ABSURD · CHLOE
TESTA · DEADWRONG
RAO · PODIA · ROI
AMSTERDAM · CHASM
ONAIR · BOATEL
RECLAME · LAPROBE
IDOL · SEIS · RAT
CURBAPPEAL · MINE
OCEANBORNE · BODY
HEARTSEASE · ESSE

68

SPYVSSPY · COCCI
THENATION · BARON
PAMELASUE · SHANT
ELECTS · OWNSUPTO
TANKS · ONTAP · PAN
ENIS · SAL · POLICE
RXS · CITYSTREETS
SATELLITE
SANATORIUMS · ELF
ONEMAN · VEE · CLEO
YOW · TIRED · CANAL
BISCOTTO · DARING
ENDON · ENDURANCE
ATARI · SCENEFOUR
NSYNC · EYETESTS

69

ASSOONAS · BLEEPS
MATAHARI · BALBOA
THATSRIDICULOUS
SLR · CLEM · REARS
SOLOS · TEENTSY
ERICA · DILLS
LIGHTAFIRE · NEW
SENSITIVENATURE
ENS · INADILEMMA
TILES · BABAR
POLENTA · FRAME
SPANS · ROLE · RIP
HEYDONTLOOKATME
AREOLE · DRILLERS
WARNED · SALMINEO

70

NETFLIX · PVCPIPE
FAIREST · AEROSOL
LUMIERE · CRUSADE
DDE · SERIESE · BUN
REZA · DRACO · JENA
AVOWS · AMA · BALKS
FINALS · BRAUN
TEESOFF · SCREWIT
HOOEY · ENDASH
SCRIP · VAC · TORTE
CLAN · DELOS · ECHO
HOI · OARLOCK · RAN
WALDORF · KUWAITI
ACOUPLE · ESOBESO
BANDSAW · DINESON

71

T	F	O	R	M	A	T	I	O	N		P	R	O	S
R	E	P	U	G	N	A	N	C	E		R	A	I	N
A	M	E	N	T	O	T	H	A	T		O	G	L	E
N	I	N	E		S	T	I	N	T		M	O	L	E
S	N	A		E	B	A	Y		Q	U	I	Z		
F	I	R	S		G	R	I	D		B	U	T	T	E
A	N	E	T		A	S	T	A	I	R	E			
T	E	A	A	C	T			P	R	E	V	I	N	
		G	U	E	S	S	S	O		N	I	C	O	
J	U	D	G	E		C	A	W	S		S	T	E	T
E	R	I	E		G	A	Y	E			A	D	A	
T	S	A	R		U	N	H	A	T		A	M	O	K
L	U	L	L		I	N	I	T	I	A	T	I	V	E
A	L	O	E		D	E	T	E	R	M	I	N	E	R
G	A	G	E		O	D	O	R	E	A	T	E	R	S

72

S	P	E	E	D	O		S	A	P	S	A	G	O
H	I	N	T	O	N		S	T	R	E	A	M	E	R
O	N	C	A	L	L		T	R	I	P	L	A	N	E
W	H	O	L	L	Y		R	O	S	S	E	T	T	I
M	O	M		A	C	T	I	V	E		P	E	E	L
A	L	I		R	H	O	D	E		G	R	U	E	L
N	E	A	P	T	I	D	E		F	A	I	R	L	Y
		A	R	L	O		M	A	R	C				
H	A	T	R	E	D		R	O	N	D	E	L	E	T
I	R	A	T	E		F	I	L	L	E		E	X	E
T	C	B	Y		V	E	B	L	E	N		S	H	E
H	A	L	F	M	I	L	E		T	H	R	O	A	T
O	D	I	O	U	S	L	Y		T	O	O	T	L	E
M	I	N	U	T	I	A	E		E	S	T	H	E	R
E	A	G	L	E	T	S			R	E	S	O	D	S

73

M	A	R	K	C	U	B	A	N		E	L	F	I	N
A	T	A	N	Y	T	I	M	E		R	O	L	L	S
C	A	M	E	R	A	B	A	G		R	O	I	L	Y
A	R	E	A			N	E	V		S	P	A	N	
W	I	N	D	S		D	A	V	E	S		F	T	C
			H	A	I			H	A	I	L	E		
R	E	A	D	I	N	G	R	A	I	L	R	O	A	D
E	X	Q	U	I	S	I	T	E	C	O	R	P	S	E
C	O	U	N	T	O	N	E	S	L	O	S	S	E	S
	T	A	K	E	N			O	E	N				
C	I	V		S	I	G	E	P		S	A	L	E	M
A	C	E	D		A	O	L			S	U	M	O	
P	I	L	E	S		D	O	N	T	I	K	N	O	W
R	S	V	P	D		O	R	I	E	N	T	A	T	E
A	M	A	T	I		T	O	M	A	T	O	R	E	D

74

F	L	A	S	H	L	I	G	H	T		A	B	C	S
A	U	C	T	I	O	N	E	E	R		B	A	H	T
V	I	R	A	L	V	I	D	E	O		S	T	A	R
A	S	E		L	E	G	S		T	S	E	T	S	E
			L	A	L	O		S	T	A	N	L	E	E
P	A	S	T	R	Y		S	K	I	N	T	E	S	T
E	N	T	R	Y		T	W	E	E	D		M	C	C
P	D	A	S		T	R	I	E	R		D	E	E	R
E	S	T		A	R	E	N	T		P	E	N	N	E
L	O	I	S	L	A	N	E		L	A	S	T	E	D
E	T	C	H	A	N	T		W	O	R	K			
M	O	L	A	R	S		G	O	A	T		C	P	O
O	B	I	S		E	U	R	O	D	I	S	N	E	Y
K	E	N	T		P	R	I	Z	E	T	A	B	L	E
O	D	E	A		T	I	N	Y	D	A	N	C	E	R

75

E	S	T	E	R		E	C	O	N		D	A	Z	E
A	H	E	A	D		A	H	S	O		E	X	I	T
G	R	A	S	S	S	T	A	I	N		B	I	T	E
L	E	S	T		M	E	T	R	O	P	O	L	I	S
E	D	E	L		A	R	T	I	S	A	N			
		D	A	I	S	I	E	S		R	A	J	A	H
S	C	H		S	H	E	D		P	R	I	O	R	I
T	O	A	D	I	E	S		Q	U	O	R	U	M	S
I	D	I	O	T	S		C	U	L	T		R	S	T
R	E	R	U	N		C	A	I	S	S	O	N		
		B	O	N	A	N	Z	A		N	A	P	E	
N	E	X	T	T	O	L	A	S	T		A	L	L	A
A	C	M	E		M	A	S	H	E	D	P	E	A	S
C	H	A	R		A	S	T	O		C	A	S	T	E
L	O	S	S		S	H	A	W		C	R	E	E	L

The New York Times
Crossword Puzzles

The #1 name in crosswords

Available at your local bookstore or online at nytimes.com/nytstore

St. Martin's Griffin

Printed in Great Britain
by Amazon

52015489R00056